THE
MASTER

The MASTER
A Life of Jesus

JOHN POLLOCK

VICTOR BOOKS®
A DIVISION OF SCRIPTURE PRESS PUBLICATIONS INC.
USA CANADA ENGLAND

Recommended Dewey Decimal Classification: 232.901
Suggested Subject Heading: LIFE OF JESUS

Library of Congress Catalog Card Number: 84-52028
ISBN: 0-89693-315-6

IN MEMORY OF
MICHAEL

Contents

Foreword 11

PART ONE:
DISCOVERY IN GALILEE. 13
  1. Companions of the Road 15
  2. The Amazing Sabbath 21
  3. "Blasphemy" 31
  4. The Customs Official 39
  5. The Call in the Hills 47
  6. Out of the Deep 53
  7. "Who Can He Be?" 61
  8. "It Is Time to Wake Up!" 69
  9. A Contrast in Compassion 75
 10. No Going Back 81
 11. To Make Him a King 87

PART TWO:
DEATH IN JERUSALEM 99
 12. The Mountain 101
 13. On the Road 111
 14. A Man Born Blind 121
 15. Lazarus 131
 16. The Last Approach 137
 17. Royal Entry 147
 18. Courts of the Temple 157
 19. The Upper Room 167
 20. The Garden 177
 21. "I Have Condemned Innocent Blood" 185
 22. "Away with Him!" 193
 23. The Lonely Hill 205

PART THREE:
GLORIOUS MORNING 215
 24. The Empty Tomb 217
 25. With You Always 229

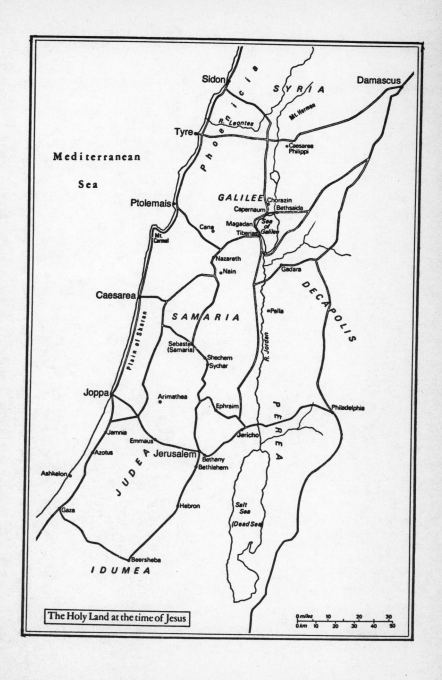

The Holy Land at the time of Jesus

Foreword

I count myself among John Pollock's greatest fans; his writings have had a tremendous impact on my life. In my early days as a Christian, I studied the Book of Acts using John's *The Apostle* as a commentary. His profile of William Wilberforce fueled my desire to emulate this great social reformer and biblical crusader of the nineteenth century; John's writings about the Siberian Seven made my heart beat as one with those of our brothers and sisters behind the Iron Curtain. John's body of work has contributed invaluable role models for the worldwide Christian community, by drawing upon the great classic stories of the heroes of the faith from the pages of Scripture and history.

But in this volume John Pollock has undertaken the greatest story of all. For in it he sketches, with love, faithfulness, and sensitivity, the life of the One whose mandates have compelled those he has profiled to live their obedient lives of faith: the Master, Jesus Christ.

In much the same way that the Gospels communicate the simplicity and power of our Lord's days on earth, John Pollock's narrative makes Christ accessible, alive, personal. For the Christian and the thoughtful nonbeliever alike, this book points the way to the Christ who lived among men, worked miracles in the dusty towns of Judea, shared God's power with a small band of ragged followers, and then took on the disgrace of death upon the Roman Empire's most degrading form of execution: the cross.

Pollock's depiction of that grisly death on our behalf points then to the victory and power of the event which transforms our lives today—the Resurrection.

So this book is a great recounting of the greatest drama of all time—and the grand paradox of God become a man, turning the ways and wisdom of this world upside down. John Pollock has faithfully depicted the person of Christ, faithfully adhered to his words; the reader cannot help but know Christ better after reading this book.

It's my prayer that this book will be used as a great tool, as have John Pollock's other works, evoking the Master, drawing others toward His love and light. It is that Light which still shines in the darkness, and can never be quenched.

CHARLES W. COLSON
Founder, Prison Fellowship,
Washington, D.C.

Part One
DISCOVERY IN GALILEE

One
COMPANIONS
OF THE ROAD

John had been aware of Jesus from his childhood. From snatches of talk between his parents, Zebedee and Salome, he knew that an element of mystery surrounded his cousin's birth; it was even rumored that Joseph was not Jesus' father, yet Salome spoke of her sister as a person of exceptional sweetness and purity.

Jesus had been born at Bethlehem, in the south, where Mary and Joseph had traveled from Nazareth because of the Roman census. When they arrived, every lodging was full and Mary thus had an experience more usual to the very poor: she gave birth to her firstborn in a stable and used a manger for his cradle. Then they had fled with the infant to Egypt to escape one of King Herod's atrocities and had not returned to Galilee until after Herod's death.

Since Jesus grew up in the hills at Nazareth and his cousins at Capernaum on the lake, the boys hardly met in their earlier years. The times were troubled. The revolt led by Judas the Galilean brought fighting in both their neighborhoods and afterward the grisly sight of men crucified at every crossroad. The land then became more tranquil and the two households could join the pilgrimage to Jerusalem for the annual Passover festival the year both boys were about twelve. Joseph and Mary spread word that Jesus was missing from the pilgrim caravan on their journey home. They hurried anxiously back up the hilly, dangerous road and found him in the Temple, listening and asking questions of the scribes and rabbis, who were astonished at his understanding.

The boys had all received the usual education; they could read and write their mother tongue, Aramaic, and could talk a bit in the common form of Greek. They had learned the meaning of great passages in the Hebrew Bible and could recite phrases. But as the years of their youth and early manhood went by, occasional contacts showed that Jesus, a carpenter by trade, had an exceptional grasp of their ancient Jewish faith.

John's religion, on the other hand, was that of any plain Jew: its unending demands hedged and shaped his life and blurred his joys. He must attend synagogue every Sabbath, hear the prayers, and sit through the Scripture readings and the address, generally a compilation from commentaries and traditions. He must attempt to keep every jot and tittle of the Law of Moses, but John being high-spirited and rather tempestuous, knew how often he failed. Yet he could imagine no other way. It was rooted in history. John was proud to be a Jew and scorned the Gentiles who crossed his path.

These were too many. When John was in his early twenties, Herod the Tetrarch, ruler of Galilee, a client state under the Romans, built a new capital city above the lakeshore a few miles south of Capernaum and named it Tiberias in honor of the emperor and peopled it mainly with Greeks or Gentiles. Even nearer home, across the Jordan into the next client state, the ruler rebuilt and enlarged a sleepy fishing village and named it Bethsaida Julius, after Caesar. It became Greek rather than Jewish in speech and customs, but this had a happy consequence for John: two Jewish brothers, Simon and Andrew, who had been born in Bethsaida, moved to the more congenial Capernaum. They were burly and virile and became partners with James and John in Zebedee's fishing business.

Little did John and the other three fishermen realize that their lives would be intertwined with the carpenter of Nazareth. Zebedee was prosperous: he supplied fish to landlocked Jerusalem, so that John was known to the household of the high priest and to other notables; but Jesus' family at Nazareth was poor, for Mary was now a widow. The two households, the one on the lake and the other in the hills, drifted apart.

Then, in the early winter of A.D. 27-28 when John was turning thirty years of age, an extraordinary rumor swept the shores of the Sea of Galilee. A new prophet had arisen out of the Judean wilderness.

John, like all Jews, had clung to the age-old hope that one day the Messiah (or Christ) would come to rescue the nation. This hope burned low: the last prophet to foretell Him had lived nearly four centuries back. No word of God could be heard except ritual readings, veiled by the mutterings of scribes.

But now, from Jerusalem and its countryside, from Galilee and beyond the Jordan, crowds flocked to the barren lands where the river flowed into the Dead Sea, in a mass movement not seen in living memory. Farmers and vinedressers were free to go because that Jewish year (running from late March) was a sabbatical—the one in every seven when the land must lie fallow and the vines unpruned. Fishermen worked during a sabbatical, but when reports grew that this prophet was the forerunner of the Messiah, or was even Christ himself, John and his brother and their partners, Simon and Andrew, left their nets. They walked south, caught up in events which would link John's life forever to his cousin. No word had come about Jesus: he remained in Nazareth, apparently unmoved by the stir.

At a ford of the Jordan, John became part of a huge crowd listening to words of fire. "Repent!" cried the prophet, "for the kingdom of heaven is near." The man had a ruggedness about him. His camel-hair sackcloth, secured by a leather belt, marked him as an ascetic. And he insisted that he was only the forerunner foretold by the Prophet Isaiah: "A voice of one calling in the wilderness, 'Prepare the way for the Lord.'" Another and a greater was coming; and to escape his judgment they must confess their sins, repent, and be baptized in the river as a symbol of being forgiven.

When the Baptist ended each sermon, he strode toward the river's edge and stood in the shallows while hundreds pressed forward to take their turns. In Galilee, James and John may have seen the solemn immersion of a Gentile convert who went under the water to mark his entry into God's people, but no Jew was ever immersed. John did not hesitate. With his brother and their two partners, he waited under the sun until at last he stood before the Baptist. John the Baptist placed a strong hand on John, son of Zebedee, who humbled himself and bowed his knees in the muddy river until the rush of water sounded in his ears.

Toward the end of that winter, when the crowds were

thinning, Jesus came from Nazareth, almost unnoticed, and was baptized after overruling the Baptist's protests. John did not see him or hear what happened. Then Jesus disappeared.

Nearly six weeks later the Baptist saw Jesus return, lean and sunburned and like a man who had emerged from a profound and costly experience which others could not share. The Baptist at once pointed him out publicly as the great one he heralded; but few took note of a young sun-burned Galilean who did not fit their expectations. Next day John and Andrew were at the Baptist's side when he again pointed Jesus out. John recognized the cousin he had scarce-ly seen since boyhood, and the Galileans shyly approached Jesus.

He welcomed them to the booth where he stayed.

Jesus was thirty years old, much the age of John, and had a well-formed body and a strikingly handsome and open face, with a fringe of beard in the usual way. Instead of a towering judge with blazing eyes, they found him a man like themselves, with a harmony of gentleness and strength which so captivated them that Andrew immediately told his brother Simon, "We have found the Messiah!" Andrew hardly real-ized what his discovery implied, nor where it would lead them, but Simon hurried to meet Jesus. Jesus summed him up in a moment: "You shall be called Rock"—*Cephas* in Aramaic, *Petros* in Greek. Thus Peter received his name.

John and James and Andrew and Peter left the banks of the Jordan with Jesus. The Baptist encouraged their change of allegiance without trace of jealousy, saying: "He must become greater; I must become less." Jesus had collected two other disciples, Philip of Bethsaida and Nathanael of Cana, each profoundly impressed by their first encounter despite Nathanael's prejudice against anyone from Nazareth.

They set out together, climbing the pilgrim path to the

eastern plateau; here they took the great road that ran south and north through a country more fertile and wooded than it would become in later centuries.

To the numerous travelers who passed them, they seemed a small party of disciples with their rabbi, a sight almost as common as a camel caravan or a posse of soldiers.

They spent the night at a roadside village. Leaving the great highway to descend again into the Jordan Valley, they walked on, in a glorious morning of friendship with no cloud of suffering on their horizon, and climbed into the hills of Galilee.

Then came the wedding at Cana of Galilee when Jesus turned water into wine. John wrote long afterward: "He revealed his glory and his disciples believed in him."

In after years John would dwell lovingly on their earlier days together and understand their meaning; but when Jesus returned to Nazareth John left him. For reasons unknown, there is a break in the story. During the winter of A.D. 29, one year after they had followed the crowds to the Baptist, the partners, John and James and Peter and Andrew, were back at their fishing; Jesus had returned to Nazareth.

In a sense, their friendship would need to begin again.

Two
THE AMAZING SABBATH

The Lake of Galilee sparkled in the spring sunshine which touched scores of sails as boats darted back and forth in trade or slowly trawled. Across the water, deep blue under a cloudless sky, the towns and villages of the eastern shore looked clear in the afternoon light, with the low hills behind them, well wooded in those years before the War of the Great Rebellion. To the north, the snow-covered summit of Mount Hermon showed hazily in the distance.

John had no eyes for scenery as he sat in the family fishing boat, drawn up on the barren stony shore, with his father and James and the hired men. John's mind was not on work either. They were preparing for the night's fishing, and James, as the elder brother, repeatedly rebuked him for tangling nets or missing a hole or ignoring seaweed which should have been washed away. John's thoughts were in a whirl. Jesus had come down from Nazareth, and John did not know whether to be glad or afraid.

First had come news that Herod had imprisoned the Baptist, silencing a mighty voice. Then travelers came into Capernaum with reports that Jesus was on the move and creating a stir wherever he went. At Nazareth they had flung him out of the synagogue. Elsewhere, they praised him and recounted his doings with awe. John had heard these rumors and tales as the spring days warmed up. On the lake at night, steering the ship or pulling in the trawl or jumping to his father's commands, he had thought long and hard. He wanted, yet dreaded, to see Jesus again. During the months of discipleship the previous year, John had remained his own master, despite growing admiration for Jesus, and had come and gone as he pleased. But he knew there might come a moment when he must pledge his allegiance forever, or go his own way.

He tangled a net again. James shouted at him.

Nearby, the other vessel of the partnership rested on the beach. Simon Peter and Andrew had prepared their deep-water trawls for the night and now stood in the shallows, stripped to their loincloths, adjusting a bell-shaped net to catch inshore fish.

Suddenly John heard a familiar voice. He looked up from his net. Jesus stood a few feet away on the shore, and behind him stood Peter and Andrew, their working clothes flung hurriedly over their burly near-naked bodies, their hair tousled and a look of adventure on their faces. Jesus' own face was shadowed by the usual flowing headdress to keep off the sun, but John could see that he smiled. His physique was slighter than that of the brothers, but his authority over them was plain. John realized by instinct that Jesus had summoned them to follow him. They had obeyed with a boyish zest which took no account of hazards ahead.

Jesus called out to James and John, "Follow me!" The moment of decision had come.

James flung down the net and leaped over the gunwale. John looked at a startled Zebedee and the hired hands. He thought of his mother, Salome, and knew she would approve. He delayed no longer. That night Zebedee took out the fishing boat without his sons.

Neither John nor Peter ever disclosed where Jesus took them nor what he taught that first day when they were together again, but at this stage he did not wish them to abandon livelihood or home. Peter went back to his wife and family each night while Jesus probably was the guest of Salome. With Friday sunset came the Sabbath, to be kept strictly as a day of rest until sunset on the Saturday. No Jew might labor: the twinkling lights on the lake at night and the sails by day would be those of Gentile boats, working out from Tiberias, Bethsaida, or the eastern shore.

A stillness hung over Capernaum when John and James, their parents, and Jesus set out on Saturday morning down the black paved streets between houses of equally dark stone. They could hear nothing but the patter of feet from all directions. Jews must walk briskly toward their synagogue, as proof of eagerness for worship, and by law every man, woman, and child should attend. The dreariness of the services prompted neighbors to find an excuse, such as ritual defilement, which could release them without risk of punishment by the elders, but this Sabbath a larger crowd than usual converged on the new synagogue. This building had been built by the Roman centurion who commanded at the barracks above the town, a man who admired and supported the subject race which his brother officers despised.

Word had gone round that Jesus of Nazareth was in town

and might be invited to teach. Jairus, the president or ruler of the synagogue, was indeed waiting outside to convey the invitation. Jairus owed his position to wealth and administrative ability rather than holiness, and he had no interest in Jesus except as a respected visiting teacher who might swell the congregation.

They entered the tall, cool building with its twin colonnades of ornamented pillars. In front stood the platform and the covered ark, which housed the scrolls. The women and small children took one side and the men and boys the other, and they all sat through the prayers and stood to recite their age-old testimony of faith in the one God. At last the *hazzan* (synagogue-keeper) walked to the ark, selected a scroll, and handed it to Jesus as he stood on the platform. Jesus unrolled it, and according to custom, he read the passage in Hebrew while the people struggled to follow a language they no longer spoke. Then he began his paraphrase and comments in their mother tongue, Aramaic.

John had heard Jesus preach and was not surprised that the congregation sat riveted. Other teachers would place before their hearers a long succession of obscure opinions by eminent rabbis until the original text lay buried. But Jesus ignored learned expounders of the past. Speaking with simplicity, he brought the passage alive and transformed it with new meaning on his own authority, "You have heard it said. . . . But I say to you. . . . "

They hung on his words. It was forbidden to exclaim aloud or interrupt a synagogue address, but John could sense their amazement, and that Jesus was making some of his neighbors uncomfortable with his insistent theme: "Repent! The kingdom of God is here, in your presence, at this moment. Repent and believe the Good News!"

Suddenly a great cry rang through the building. A man on

one of the benches yelled in a high-pitched voice, throwing at Jesus the age-old phrase of challenge and taunt to an enemy, *"What have we to do with you,* Jesus of Nazareth?"

The people were horrified. They recognized the man's voice and wondered how he had slipped in, for by his staring eyes and strange ways they knew him to be in the grip of a demon, an unclean evil spirit, and should have been excluded from the congregation. He had defiled them by his presence and now was spoiling the sermon. They tried to suppress him: this rabbi from Nazareth might attempt a lengthy exorcism later but not here in the synagogue. Meanwhile, the man must be silenced.

But he yelled the more. "Jesus of Nazareth! I know who you are—the Holy One of God." Now he had added blasphemy, the people believed. They hoped the preacher would ignore him.

Jesus stopped. He looked in the man's direction and spoke in a stern, emphatic voice. "Be quiet! And come out of him at once!"

The man shuddered violently. With a loud shriek, he fell to the floor.

A few moments later the people could hardly believe their eyes. The man had picked himself up and now sat quietly with an intelligent look, which none had seen on his face for years. As Jesus resumed his sermon, the man listened, plainly unaware that he had made a noise.

When the sermon ended and the congregation spilled out, they could not contain their excitement. "It is something new," they were saying. "It is his authority which is amazing—he taught us on his own authority and not like the scribes." "Did you see his power over that demon? He told it to go and it obeyed; that is the most amazing of all."

Jesus slipped away. With John and James, he had promised to share the Sabbath meal at the home of Peter and his wife and Andrew. All over Capernaum delicious meals had been prepared the previous day to make the Sabbath delightful, and the women had nothing to do after synagogue but serve their menfolk. Peter's wife, however, was not at the synagogue because her mother, who kept house for them, had retired to bed with a fever, and she had stayed behind.

Peter hurried ahead while the others walked at the slow pace which traditionally symbolized sorrow that divine service had ended. The lake lay placid before them through a forest of the masts and furled sails of the larger ships riding at anchor.

When Jesus and his friends reached the house on the strand and entered the little courtyard which it enclosed, they found Peter and his wife in distress. She wrung her hands and brushed away tears as she told Jesus that her mother's fever had risen violently. And the meal had not been laid. Instead of the honor and pleasure they had intended to give him, he would sit down to their sadness and fear.

"Take me to her," said Jesus. They all went upstairs.

The old woman lay in a feverish sweat, already a little delirious. As Jesus bent over her, he seemed to John the very picture of physical well-being, to whom this fever was a personal affront, not to be tolerated in one of his friends.

Jesus said something which sounded like a rebuke, not to the patient but to the fever. He gripped her hand and helped her off the bed. She stood up. Her hot face cooled in an instant. Instead of tottering in a feeble convalescence, she was her usual brisk self and hustled them out of the room while she washed and dressed. She hurried to the kitchen. The men soon sat down to the happiest of meals.

Afterward, a stillness descended on Capernaum as every

household rested until the sun dropped behind the hills in the west and the Sabbath was nearly over. Suddenly Jesus and his friends heard sounds of movement from neighboring houses and streets. John crossed the courtyard and looked out. By the light of the sunset, he was amazed to see the roadway filling with people limping or bandaged or coughing or fevered. Word had gone round of the incident in the synagogue, and a rumor was spreading quickly about Peter's mother-in-law. The pent-up misery of a country town was on the move. Sufferers might walk the short distance to Peter's house without desecrating the Sabbath, and since they had assumed that Jesus would never heal until it ended, because to heal would be to work, they had wanted to be ready. As darkness fell, men arrived with stretchers or with beds, not having dared carry one before sundown lest they be reported to the elders.

Jesus walked into the road. To John's astonishment, he healed the first cases by a touch or by a word. Soon his four friends were struggling to organize sufferers and keep off sightseers, both of which increased dramatically when patients whom Jesus had cured ran around the town spreading the news. Peter and John could recognize sick neighbors. Soon strangers outnumbered them because Capernaum was a dormitory for visitors to the healing springs beyond Tiberias, a city which pious Jews shunned for its defiling Gentile atmosphere.

Young men set up torches to light the scene. The crowd spilled over to the beach; some of the ablebodied even climbed the rigging of nearby ships to get a view. Compared with the multitudes who thronged him later, this crowd was small, but the noise sounded extraordinary; groans and pleas, the cries of epileptics foaming on the ground, shouts from those in the grip of evil demons, until Jesus silenced them with peremptory words which seemed to express equally his hatred of evil and his pleasure at the release of victims.

The scene left an indelible memory on those who were cured, and on sightseers. The centurion who had given the town its synagogue had hurried down from the barracks at the hubbub. Riot troops were not needed, but he stayed to watch, his military mind impressed by a sense that Jesus exercised power as representative of a mighty authority, which the forces of evil recognized and obeyed.

Another sightseer, variously named Levi or Matthew, saw it differently. Matthew at that time was a somewhat disreputable and unpopular character who did well for himself as collector of customs at the border outside the town. He had an excellent knowledge of the Hebrew prophets, however. This night scene reminded him of Isaiah's prophecy of the Suffering Servant: "He took our infirmities on himself and carried away our diseases."

John, keeping close to Jesus to protect him from the press of bodies, saw by his face how much it cost him. John was distressed for his Master yet excited by awareness of elemental, apparently inexhaustible power; and he was moved beyond words as he watched Jesus at work. John had seen him heal particular cases; tonight he healed all who came, and though neither John nor his friends described symptoms in the detail which they gave to some later incidents, John marveled at Jesus' compassion. Just as he had entered fully into the merriment at Cana, so now he became part of the suffering.

After the last patient, Jesus gave a quick smile to his friends, lay down on Peter's floor, and fell asleep. John walked home with James, climbed to his loft, and went to bed. But he could not sleep. His brain refused to rest as he tried to fathom an amazing man and extraordinary events.

John knew nothing of a crucifixion, nor of h
grave, nor of incidents to come in Jesus' life and st
Jesus' lips which countless millions down the ages w
learn at Mother's knee. He could not tell what Jesus would
do, only that he had a purpose and seemed in command of
events and of himself. There were majesty and mystery in his
character; he must be far more than a carpenter or a cousin,
yet he was approachable. John wanted to be with him and to
help him, and never to leave again.

Suddenly shouts, far away at first, penetrated the deep
sleep into which John had fallen. The voice of Peter roused
him and he rushed to the window. Dawn had broken but
the sun not yet risen.

"He has gone!" cried Peter from the street. "I came down
at dawn. . . . People are coming to the door already. . . . but
he has gone!"

...finding an empty
...ories from
...roud

Three
"BLASPHEMY!"

They hurried across the flat ground and climbed into the hills behind the town. As the sun rose to their right, they could see vessels returning after the night's work or hoisting sail to find the early morning shoals. Below, they caught glints on the spears and armor of soldiers parading in the barracks.

They passed fields which had been scraped from the poor soil. They scrambled up basalt rocks and beside the mouths of ancient caves. Peter had an instinct as to where they might find Jesus. John panted behind him with James and Andrew, and they climbed for nearly an hour, eating handfuls of raisins which John had taken from the larder. Then Peter stopped and listened. In quietness broken only by the cries of birds, they heard the voice of Jesus. With a glance at the others, Peter led them along the desolate hillside until they saw ahead a white figure against the basalt. They walked a little nearer, then stood transfixed.

Jesus was talking, apparently unaware of their presence. His face was lifted toward heaven and his knees were on the ground in an attitude of prayer; this was strange, for Jews always stood to pray. They were not surprised that he prayed aloud, because no man in the first century either read or prayed silently, or at least without using his lips; but Jesus was speaking to God with a familiarity which would have appalled them in anyone else. "Abba, Father," he prayed. Jesus had spoken the intimate term used by a child at home to a greatly loved parent; the liturgy addressed God formally as Father of the Children of Israel, but no individual Jew would dare call the Almighty Creator of the world "Daddy."

They eavesdropped. Jesus was asking his Father, in simple words, to bless sufferers he had healed. He offered himself for those yet to come. He spoke next of his close friends, one by one, until John realized how surely Jesus had probed their characters and failings and hopes; as Jesus prayed, John wanted to be like him in every way, and believed that this would be possible if only they kept together.

Jesus stopped praying. Rising from his knees, he turned to them and smiled. Pleasure at seeing them, forgiveness for their following him unasked, and for their eavesdropping were all in that smile, so that Peter was bold and exclaimed, "Everybody is looking for you!"

Jesus ignored the implied rebuke. And he did not turn back with them. "We shall go to other towns," he said, "so that I can preach the Good News. That is why I was sent." He began walking along the hillside in the direction of Chorazin, and because he had eaten nothing, they pressed the rest of their raisins upon him, and stopped to drink when they found a spring.

The next weeks were unforgettable, as they went from

village to village and town to town. Jesus avoided "Greek" cities, nor would he return to Nazareth where his boyhood neighbors had applauded his preaching and then tried to murder him when he spoke home truths; but day after day he and his disciples walked the lanes and roads of Galilee. Sometimes they slept outdoors, but often a family offered welcome. Not having prepared for the journey, they carried no change of clothes, nor extra cloaks or sandals, and Jesus accepted hospitality and necessities as their due, but always with gratitude and courtesy.

When tired he was not cross. He never seemed to hurry yet never was lazy. His happiness, his endurance, unselfishness, and his peace of mind made every day a joy. John would never have believed that a man could be faultless, until he traveled with Jesus. Religious neighbors who boasted themselves as nearly perfect were insufferable, but Jesus made a delightful companion. Plainly, he felt the same pressures as his friends, yet always his reaction was right.

They noticed another most curious facet of his character, all the more surprising in view of his humility. When he went aside in the early mornings to some deserted spot where he could pray, and they escorted him and kept vigil a stone's throw off, they never once heard him confess sins or utter a prayer of penitence.

Whenever he entered a new place, he would ask to use the synagogue, whether a noble building as at Chorazin or little more than a shack in small villages; and because his fame had spread round the district and beyond, a crowd would gather at once.

On Sabbaths he took part in the liturgy. Often he would unroll the scroll of Isaiah until he found the prophecy which he had read out at Nazareth the day they had tried to destroy him: "The Spirit of the Lord is upon me, because he has anointed me to preach Good News to the poor. He has sent me to proclaim freedom for the prisoner and recovery of sight for the blind, to release the oppressed, to proclaim the year of the Lord's favor." When he ended his reading, all waited in intense silence to learn how he would expound the text. Jesus at once told them without apology or hesitation that the prophecy had come true as they listened: soon they saw proof as they brought him their sick.

One incident enlarged the crowds until they were nearly out of hand; yet it had filled his four close friends with horror at first. They were walking with Jesus toward one of the towns when they saw a man in rags and with an unkempt beard. They knew at once the obligatory signs—leper—and he should have shouted, "Unclean! Unclean!" to warn them.

The Greek word related to several skin diseases. Not all were as grievous or contagious as leprosy, but every sufferer was regarded as ritually unclean, and must avoid inhabited areas and distance himself from passers-by. The disciples drew back in disgust and fear when this one hurried nearer with his hideous bleached and flaking skin. He knelt down in the road less than a foot in front of Jesus and bowed his face into the dust in an attitude of abject humility and sorrow.

The disciples would have hustled him away before he could harm their Master, but they dared not touch the man. They were in a dilemma: unable to help, unwilling to run. They loathed the creature.

The leper looked up, covered with gray dust, which stood out against the whiteness of the infected skin. He pleaded, "Lord, if you want to, you can make me clean."

Jesus, who seemed unaware of his friends' fears or loathing, answered tenderly with unconcealed compassion, "Of course, I am willing!"

John had never known Jesus to heal a leper. John did not doubt his power nor, unlike the sufferer, his willingness; but John fervently hoped that Jesus would avoid contact, like the Prophet Elisha long ago, when he healed the Syrian general Naaman from a distance.

Jesus put out his hand and touched the man. The disciples were aghast. Not only had Jesus broken the religious laws and rendered himself unclean, he had endangered his health.

Jesus said, "Be clean!"

The Scriptures told how Naaman's flesh, when he obeyed Elisha, "came again like unto the flesh of a little child and he was clean." John had never expected to see such a thing take place before his eyes. As the disciples stared, the kneeling man's skin grew soft and took on its natural color. A look of intense gratitude spread across his face.

Then Jesus, so tender a moment before, spoke sharply to him: "Don't say a word to anyone!" Jesus ordered him to go to a priest for ritual discharge as a cured leper. He would take offerings and show his body and be pronounced clean. And he must stay silent.

The man disobeyed. He made the land ring with the story of his instant cure by Jesus of Nazareth. The sensation was enormous. Wherever Jesus went the crowds converged in such numbers that he could no longer preach in synagogues or even enter the towns, but must preach and heal in the pastures or on hillsides. At last he returned to Capernaum with his friends, very privately, early one morning before the town was astir.

Shortly afterward, John needed to revise profoundly his understanding of Jesus.

Dignitaries from Jerusalem had knocked at Peter's door. Their clothes, as well as their way of walking and speaking, showed them to be Pharisees—the "separated ones" who regarded themselves as the true guardians of Jewish religious purity, though many cared for outward display more than sincerity, and their ostentatious prayers at street corners were a byword. With these Jerusalem men came local Pharisees and some scribes, men who interpreted and upheld the Law of Moses in its every detailed requirement, but often were unpopular for refusal to help carry the moral burdens which they laid on men's shoulders.

Pharisees and scribes could ruin a man. Their appearance in Peter's courtyard sent a tremor through the household. Peter took the deputation to the upper guest chamber and told Jesus, who rested in his room, and they walked together, with John, along the narrow covered gallery which was the usual upper passageway of such a house, and entered the guest chamber. While the mother-in-law served refreshments, Jesus conversed with his formidable callers. They asked searching questions.

Their arrival had alerted the neighbors that Jesus was home. Several entered the yard and sat quietly below in the shade of the gallery, ready to wait all day to hear him. They were soon joined by so many others that Peter looked out at the stir, and Jesus courteously told the Pharisees and scribes that he must preach. Since their purpose was to test his teaching, they welcomed the opportunity to listen and moved closer to the balcony when he stepped outside.

They heard the crowd's noisy welcome. Jesus leaned against the rails of the gallery, protected from the sun by its overhanging tiles, and began to preach. Peter and John stood near him, half listening, half nervously watching the scribes and Pharisees. Jesus' voice had a warm attractive timbre and even when modulated to address a small crowd in a confined space it carried well, until townsfolk in nearby streets hurried nearer and pressed into the entrance, pushing until the yard could contain no more. Latecomers jammed the entrance and spread across the roadway.

Jesus had preached in the shade for about half an hour when John noticed a sudden ray of sunshine on his Master's face. A moment more and the light increased and some dust fell to the floor. John looked up and to his astonishment saw tiles being lifted one by one until a space had opened over the gallery between the projecting eaves and the house wall. Jesus stopped. The crowd below and the disciples on the gallery watched, fascinated. Four brawny fishermen had been working unnoticed from over the low parapet which protected the flat roof of the house. They now lifted a pallet, secured at each corner with ropes, and let it down gently until it rested at Jesus' feet. On the pallet lay a misshapen man. He was not old, but his legs were drawn up stiffly at an unnatural angle, his arms lay rigid at his sides, and he looked up at Jesus with an expression of pleading and fear.

John realized at once what had happened. The four fishermen had intended to carry their paralyzed friend into the house and ask Jesus to heal him. Blocked by the crowd at the entrance, unable even to see Jesus, they had cannily gone down the street, begged permission to ascend to a flat rooftop and then had carried the man above the main block over each dividing parapet, until above Peter's. They could not dig through the beaten earth above the rooms without causing a cascade of dirt, but to remove the projecting tiles of the gallery was simple for sailors, who smiled with triumph as they saw their friend right beside Jesus.

Jesus smiled back, plainly delighted at their faith. Then he gazed down at the wreck of the man. Silence fell on the crowd as they watched from below. The Pharisees and the scribes leaned forward intently from inside the guest chamber. John waited. He had long abandoned any attempt to discover how Jesus penetrated a stranger's mind or could know his history.

Jesus spoke. "Son," he said, "your sins are forgiven you."

The Pharisees almost leaped from their places. They were appalled. Again, Jesus seemed to divine unspoken thoughts, for as John groped in his mind to understand what appalled them, Jesus turned and said to them: "Why are you thinking these things? Which is easier? To say to this paralyzed man, 'Your sins are forgiven you,' or to say, 'Get up, take your pallet and walk?' So that you shall know that the Son of man has authority on earth to forgive sins—" He spoke to the man again. "I am telling you now. Get up! Take up your pallet! Go home!"

The Pharisees and scribes gripped each other with amazement and anger as the man, his eyes fixed on Jesus, straightened one leg, then the other. He placed a once-rigid arm on the ground and stood up. Perfectly strong, he leaned down with a bemused expression and rolled up the pallet, ropes and all, then stretched himself. A broad grin of pure pleasure crossed his face. He took one step, another, and walked along the gallery as a great roar went up from the crowd, a shout of praise to God. "We have never seen anything like this," they were saying as Peter escorted the man downstairs into the yard. People made way for him, right out on to the street, to join his friends who had run and leaped across the roofs and down the way they had come.

The crowd broke up in excitement. But the Pharisees left without another word.

Afterward, John asked Jesus what these men had been thinking. Jesus looked straight at him. "They thought like this," he replied. " 'Blasphemy! This man blasphemes! Who can forgive sins *but God alone?*' "

Four
THE CUSTOMS OFFICIAL

John puzzled how one who was good and humble could claim to be God. John, Peter, and their brothers believed already that Jesus was the Messiah foretold by the prophets, but the prophets had not seemed to suggest that God himself, the Creator of heaven and earth, would come to his world; the Messiah would be a human being whom he anointed. Learned commentators even taught that several "Anointed Ones" might appear, for the Mighty King who would restore Israel's power and glory could hardly be the Suffering Servant too.

This was confusing to a fisherman, but not as perplexing as Jesus' announcement to the paralyzed man: "Son, your sins are forgiven." As the Pharisees saw, none can forgive sins but God alone, yet Jesus was sane; he was totally honest; moreover his implied claim to at least one of the attributes of God had been endorsed when the paralyzed man stood up and walked.

John did not try to resolve the dilemma. He wanted to stay with Jesus, to listen and watch; no one in the world meant more to him or, he was sure, to Peter, James, and Andrew. Jesus would make everything plain in time.

Meanwhile, fresh surprises were in store. One day they were threading their way along the road which led from Capernaum toward Bethsaida. A late spring rain had kept the listening crowds away, and now the weather was cloudy; Mount Hermon had disappeared, and the hills above the eastern shore looked distant. Jesus evidently had a purpose, though he had not disclosed it, for otherwise he would not have chosen the busiest route, where mule and camel trains befouled the paving stones and masters cursed the foot passengers whose bundles of belongings or merchandise got in the way. Drovers behind flocks of sheep and goats, and horsemen trotting or cantering on official business made the walk slow and a trifle hazardous. And all except officials were congealed into an impatient mass when the road reached the border customs post. Every bundle had to be unloaded, every sheep and goat counted; even clothing might be liable for tax.

At the head desk of the post sat Matthew, unperturbed by the noise, unaffected by the impatience and suppressed fury of those whose goods and persons he taxed. Like any taxgatherer or "publican" in Palestine, he was detested by most of his neighbors as an indirect agent of the occupying power, who made a comfortable living from the percentage he took for himself and from the bribes of those he passed unchecked. To the devout, he was an outcast, defiled by consorting with Gentiles and by too frequent handling of the pagan coinage with its image of Caesar. No one believed that a taxgatherer could be honest.

Jesus stopped at the customs post and watched. The expression on his face was not of disapproval so much as sympathy. He knew Matthew's interest in the Scriptures and especially the prophecies, knew of his presence when the sick had been healed during the evening of that Sabbath early in the spring. But the disciples grew restless: a publican was no fit companion for a man of God. The sooner Jesus continued his walk the better.

Matthew was absorbed in checking his underlings' work, in calculating and collecting. He took some time to be aware of Jesus. He looked up and their eyes met.

"Follow me," said Jesus.

After an almost imperceptible pause, Matthew decided to abandon his livelihood and ordered his chief assistant to carry on. Jesus turned back toward Capernaum, and there was almost a laugh in his tone as he told the disciples to welcome their new colleague, for their faces displayed a mixture of surprise, distaste, and admiration. They were surprised that Jesus should choose such a disciple. John knew himself to be a lusty young man with a hot temper, but he had not followed a disreputable profession nor consorted with men and women who broke the Law of Moses. Yet he admired Matthew's courage. When the fishermen had responded to Jesus' call, they had not lost their fishing boats, and had gone out on the lake several times since, but Matthew would be dismissed from the customs service forthwith. He had nothing left but savings.

John soon discovered that these savings were to help Jesus, in a glorious gesture before Matthew took the road as his disciple.

Matthew had been walking beside Jesus in front of their group, talking earnestly. Jesus had nodded, and when they reached the rather grand suburb where Matthew lived, they parted, Matthew to his home, the others toward Peter's house near the lake. Jesus told them to be ready in their best robes in time to return to Matthew's for dinner.

John had never entered the house of such a man, who to all good Jews was a sinner. Jesus, however, plainly felt no shame as they walked in, and John had already noticed the curious fact that any place which Jesus entered would soon reflect his character rather than its own. The house looked roomy and luxurious, with silk hangings and richly worked brocade on the couches—all bought, assumed John, by grinding the faces of travelers on the highways in Herod's name. Jesus had told the disciples as they approached the house that Matthew would sell everything, giving part to the poor and part toward supporting themselves as they walked those very roads in the months to come. If Matthew had a wife and family (which is uncertain), enough would be held back to keep them in simplicity.

Matthew bade them recline in comfort beside tables loaded with food. The friends he had summoned at short notice to enjoy a last banquet shocked John. There were tax collectors and customs officers from Bethsaida, Capernaum, and Tiberias, even a latecomer who in response to Matthew's messenger had hurried in from Chorazin, leaving his donkey lathered in sweat to recover in the shade of the garden behind; every one of these was a despised publican. Others were sinners who had cut themselves off from the synagogue by marrying Gentiles. In the shadows among the women, John thought he saw a prostitute; publicans certainly consorted with such, and Matthew probably had been no exception. Scarcely a man among his friends had not committed adultery, for they lived more like Gentiles than Jews. Some had doubtless worshiped in pagan temples.

Jesus received Matthew's lavish hospitality with enjoyment, and the hearts of those present went out to him. They listened to his words about repentance and purity and the kingdom which had come among them. Some became his followers, sensing that only by keeping near him would they resist the pull to a prostitute's bed or cease to rob the poor. Others looked wistful, thanked Matthew for the delightful banquet, and left. A few scarcely hid their contempt.

As the disciples came out into the street, while Jesus lingered inside with guests who sought his counsel, they were met by an angry group of Pharisees and scribes. News of the banquet had reached them as an almost unbelievable rumor that Jesus had not only entered the house of a man of bad repute but was eating with disgraceful companions. Since they had honored Jesus by allowing him to teach in the synagogue, his behavior reflected on their respectability. They threw a question at Peter and John: "Why does your Master eat with publicans and sinners?"

The question held menace, for a teacher who kept company with sinners could be silenced, might even be excommunicated, with his disciples. It held concern too, for some of the Pharisees were merciful men who cared deeply for their countrymen and believed that Jesus had a genuine gift for talking about God in a way that the simple and the poor could understand. If he cut himself from the mainstream of the nation's religious life, he would lose influence.

"Why does he eat and drink with taxgatherers and sinners?" they asked again. Jesus overheard the question as he came out into the street. He answered at once: "The healthy do not need the doctor! It is the sick who do. I have not come to call the righteous, but sinners." He threw in an apposite text and told them to go and learn what it meant.

He left them standing by the gate. Whether or not they

held a learned debate on his answer, they soon showed that he had not met their complaint, for wherever the disciples went with Jesus in the next few days, some of this group shadowed them. The important men from Jerusalem who had gone back to report the incident of the paralyzed man would be returning to Capernaum shortly, and the local Pharisees wished to collect evidence on which a ruling might be made, whether to endorse Jesus or to throw him out.

A day or two after Matthew's feast, the Sabbath came round and Jesus taught in the synagogue. The scribes and Pharisees sat impassive, testing his every word for error. They followed him out afterward and dogged his steps when he led the disciples through the fields behind the town toward a secluded pasture, where he wanted to teach them privately before they went back together for the Sabbath meal. John and Peter reveled in the fresh spiritual horizons his sermon had opened, but being hungry they casually exercised the wayfarer's immemorial right to pull heads of wheat from the wheat crops. Harvest was near, for the late spring rains and sun had ripened the wheat fast in the low-lying lands beside the lake. The disciples husked the grain with their hands and tossed it into their mouths.

They heard a shout from behind. An angry Pharisee hurried up to Jesus and demanded, "Why do your disciples break the Sabbath?" It took a moment to guess the man's meaning. Then it dawned on them that he rated their plucking the heads of wheat as equal to the work of harvesting by sickle, one of the thirty-nine actions prohibited on the Sabbath.

Jesus promptly rebuked the Pharisee by citing an incident in the Scriptures, followed by two breathtaking statements: "The Sabbath is made for man, not man for the Sabbath!" exclaimed Jesus. Then, using the title with which he often referred to himself, he said, "The Son of man is Lord of the Sabbath too."

Seven days later when John went with his parents to the synagogue, he saw the Jerusalem deputation in town again, prominent on the benches reserved for rulers. Behind them sat the Pharisee whom Jesus had rebuked.

Placed where Jesus would notice him when handed the sacred scroll for the reading was a stranger disfigured by a withered hand. John suspected at once that this man had been brought from outside the town as bait with which to trap Jesus. John did not doubt his Master's power to remake a shriveled hand, whether atrophied as the result of accident or deformed from birth, but he realized at once why the man had been planted there: its healing would require a major work of reconstruction—on a Sabbath Day.

When the *hazzan* invited Jesus to the reading desk, the Pharisees leaned forward and watched closely, mentally waiting to pounce. The *hazzan* offered a sacred scroll. Jesus took and unrolled it, read a passage and began to expound as if a shriveled hand meant nothing to him. Suddenly he stopped. Looking straight at the man, he commanded: "Get up, and stand here in front where everybody can see you."

The man obeyed. A hush fell on the synagogue as the tension rose. The stranger's face expressed hope mingled with doubt and embarrassment. The Pharisees pursed their lips. Jesus turned toward them and in the unemotional tone of voice which rabbis used in debate, he put to them a question in debating form: "Tell me. Which is lawful on the Sabbath Day: to do good or to do evil? To save life or to kill?"

The Pharisees declined the debate. They stayed mute, but Jesus was angry. The anger threw into sharp relief the lovelessness, the hypocrisy, and narrowness of the religious leaders who cared for the letter of the Law but not for a crippled man. John could tell that the man mattered to Jesus, and that the hardness of heart of the Pharisees distressed him equally; if only they would open to Jesus, he could heal them too.

Every eye was now on the crippled man. "Stretch out your hand,' ordered Jesus.

As the man stretched it out, a gasp of amazement passed through the congregation. No one ever described the process in detail, but all could see that a useless, shriveled hand had become strong.

Five
THE CALL
IN THE HILLS

The authorities banned Jesus from teaching in the synagogue for his flagrant breach of Sabbath regulations. They did not excommunicate him nor sentence him to be whipped, but they marked him publicly as in disgrace. Privately, they began to think of ways to murder him. Those who kept him company would lose their good names and perhaps their lives.

A few evenings later Jesus instructed Peter and John to pass the word that early next morning he would teach at a lonely spot above Capernaum. He went away by himself, ordering them on no account to follow him into the hills, while they visited or sent messages to all in the neighborhood who regularly sat at his feet. At first light they found that some had excused themselves, but seventy or eighty of the more eager were walking up the mountain, unaware why

Jesus wanted them.

When the followers arrived at the chosen little plateau, John saw Jesus on a rock looking out across the lake below, which sparkled in the summer morning sun before the heat haze blurred the view. He seemed bathed in sunshine, but as they came closer, John realized that Jesus' face and eyes shone with an inner light; he must have spent the night in prayer.

Once they had gathered round him, Jesus explained his purpose. He was about to choose twelve men to work at his side, or occasionally to go elsewhere on his behalf and learn more than he could impart to crowds.

John's heart missed a beat or two as he waited to hear whether he would be one of the Twelve. First Jesus called out Simon Peter's name, and immediately, with a characteristic touch, put Andrew's fear at rest by telling him to join his brother. When John heard his own older brother named, his doubts dissolved, and a few moments later he was with James at Jesus' side. Jesus next called the friends of the walk to Cana from Jordan's bank, Philip and Bartholomew-Nathanael; then Matthew, and five more. Only one of the Twelve was not a Galilean. His name was Judas Iscariot, "the man from Kerioth," a town on the plateau to the east of the Dead Sea. Nothing about Judas gave a hint to the eleven others that the seeds of treachery were in him.

John was almost overcome by excitement, by feelings of privilege and gratitude, and a determination to be worthy. On the other hand, Jesus conveyed the unspoken sense that the privilege of having the Twelve was his, that each was a gift entrusted to him for their sakes as much as for his. John looked around at these eleven men who henceforth would be his everyday companions. Despite his affection for Peter and Andrew and love for his own brother, and the friendship which had already grown with most of the others, he could not help contrasting them with Jesus. Several might be taller or look stronger, but morally and in wisdom they could not compare.

There was little time for such thoughts. Someone called out that masses of people were crawling, as it seemed from that height, up the trail they themselves had taken in the early morning. Jesus began to walk down the mountain toward them immediately, as if to teach the Twelve their future attitude to fellowmen. The rest followed. He chose a level space on the hillside and waited.

No one, least of all John, could fail to be moved by the happiness of the people when they saw Jesus. There were not only Galileans; those from Judea and the coastal districts and the cities beyond the Jordan could be identified by slight differences in dress and speech. Young and old, poor and a few rich, men, women, and youngsters pressed close to Jesus, eager to touch him, to tell him of their sicknesses or to bring friends and relatives who needed care or relief. It was a scene which was becoming familiar: the pressure of the sick and the healthy; the selflessness with which Jesus helped them, and the indefinable energy which came through his touch. This time there was a difference. When he had healed all patients brought to him, Jesus instructed the Twelve to settle everybody on the grass, facing a knoll. The disciples from whom he had chosen the Twelve were to be in front.

He sat on the knoll, just as previously he had sat to teach in the synagogue, and then, his voice carried clear by the breeze to the confines of the crowd, he spoke the words which would echo round the world, through all ages, as the Sermon on the Mount.

"Blessed are the poor in spirit," he began, "for theirs is the kingdom of heaven. Blessed are those who mourn, for they will be comforted. Blessed are the meek, for they will inherit the earth.

"Blessed are those who hunger and thirst for righteousness, for they will be filled. Blessed are the merciful, for they will be shown mercy. Blessed are the pure in heart, for they will see God. Blessed are the peacemakers, for they will be called sons of God. Blessed are those who are persecuted because of righteousness, for theirs is the kingdom of heaven.

"Blessed are you when men insult you, persecute you, and falsely say all kinds of evil things against you because of me. Rejoice and be glad, because great is your reward in heaven, for in the same way they persecuted the prophets who were before you."

He continued with many practical exhortations. In the months to come, he would repeat what he said, sometimes varying his words, but this Sermon on the Mount would be remembered as the essence of all that he spoke on the theme of a disciple's way of life. They listened with strict attention, committing the words to memory. Since papyrus and parchment scrolls were owned only by rich men and the synagogues and the religious schools, Jews learned at their mothers' knees to memorize. A teacher's followers took pride in treasuring the teaching without changing it. Those closest, such as Jesus' own Twelve, considered it a point of honor to reproduce their Master's gestures and the very tones of his voice and his precise words.

It was easy to listen to Jesus, for he made his points with allusions to familiar things, such as salt which has lost its saltiness, or shining lamps, or a city on a hill, like Nazareth. Urging his hearers to keep their treasure in heaven, safe from hazards, he spoke of moths and rust, and thieves who break in and steal. In teaching against worry, he spoke of the wild flowers of springtime which neither toil nor spin: "Yet Solomon in all his glory was not arrayed like one of these."

As he continued, each listener saw in the mind's eye an angry worshiper, brought up short in the Temple by the need to make peace with a brother whom he had wronged; or a pompous hypocrite shouting out his prayers so that all should admire him, and hiring a trumpeter to advertise his gifts to charity. They all saw, with laughter, a carpenter trying to remove a speck of sawdust from a workmate's eye when he could hardly see for the splinter sticking in his own. And Jesus recalled to everyone's memory the anger and weariness of a hot walk when conscripted by a Roman soldier to carry his heavy load; a soldier had the right to compel a man to go one mile. Jesus surprised them by saying, "Go with him two."

Throughout his sermon Jesus contrasted natural attitudes with a life dictated by love, righteousness, and faith. To his hearers on that day, all of whom were Jews, or Gentiles following the Jewish way, it sounded a matter of emphasis: if they did as Jesus taught, they would really fulfill the spirit of the Law of Moses. But his words would be revolutionary when taught near pagan temples in Greek and Roman cities, or in faraway lands where for centuries, when Jesus first spoke them, men had followed the Buddha or Confucius, or had worshiped Hindu gods.

Libraries of books would be written relating to the Sermon on the Mount. Every phrase would be examined and expounded. At the time, as John listened closely with Peter and their friends, he could not fail to notice that the picture held before them of a perfect man was a self-portrait. The Jesus they knew, as no others yet knew so well, was meek and humble and merciful and a peacemaker; he loved his enemies and gave freely; he never worried about food or clothes or what would happen the next day. In effect, he was instructing them to be like him. But John understood himself well enough to realize that on his own he could not reproduce Jesus' character nor live up to the standards which he set; nor, John suspected, could a single one of the audience.

The only hope was to stay in Jesus' company, strengthened by his example, perhaps growing more like him, little by little. They were young men still, and the years stretched ahead. Had not Jesus just said, "Do not worry about tomorrow"?

John pulled back his thoughts, for the sermon was rising to a climax with a vivid story. "The man," said Jesus, "who hears my words and puts them into practice is like a wise man who builds his house on a rock," laboriously hacking and digging and sweating to lay the foundation, until at last he has his house. "The rains came; the river rose; the wind blew and beat against the house. And it did not collapse because its foundation was in the rock."

Then for everyone who heard the teaching and did nothing, Jesus painted a word picture of a foolish man who built his house with speed and ease by putting the foundation into the sandy soil above the riverbed. "The rains came; the river rose; and the winds blew and beat against that house—and down it came with a crash!"

Six
OUT OF
THE DEEP

While John listened enthralled to the Sermon on the Mount, a tragedy was unfolding below at the Capernaum barracks. Its commanding officer, the pagan centurion who had built the Jewish synagogue, was in despair because his household manager, his most trusted slave, lay dying in agony from a paralysis which almost prevented his breathing. This slave was not only valuable for his command of figures but a dear friend: a relationship often found in the Roman Empire where slaves could rise to important posts.

Physicians had failed. Time was running out. Suddenly the centurion recalled the night, after reports of an exceptional crowd, he had watched the sick being healed by Jesus. Jesus had impressed him as different from the wandering miracle workers and the quacks he had met in his army life. But the more holy the man, the less he would be willing to defile himself by entering a Gentile home or meeting a Gentile's direct request, or so the centurion believed from his observation of Jewish religion. He therefore sent a message to the elders of the synagogue which he had paid for, asking them to intercede with Jesus to save the slave's life.

This put the elders in a dilemma. They had excluded Jesus from the synagogue and branded him as an undesirable character, yet they dared not deny a senior officer in Herod's service who was their own benefactor.

Hot from the descent but exhilarated by all they had heard on the mountain, the disciples were not a little surprised to find a deputation of elders welcoming Jesus to the town where they had tried to disgrace him. When they began to list the centurion's virtues, the irony of the situation could not be missed: the elders were begging a man they had rejected to help a man whom they despised, as a Gentile, whatever his generosity.

Jesus cut short their fulsome account. "I will go," he said.

As they all walked toward the barracks, a messenger must have run ahead to encourage the centurion, for another deputation met Jesus. Two or three of the centurion's friends carried an urgent message, which they gave word-for-word as from himself: "Lord, do not put yourself to trouble, for I do not deserve to have you under my roof. That is why I sent friends instead of coming to you myself. *Just say the word* and my slave will be healed! For I too act under authority. I have soldiers under me. I order one, 'Go!' and he goes, and another, 'Come!' and he comes. And I order a slave, 'Do this!' and he does it."

Though Jesus could penetrate the unspoken angry thoughts of scribes and Pharisees, he let himself appear astounded at the faith of a Gentile. He turned to the crowd at his heels and with delight in his voice said with great emphasis, "I have not found faith as strong as this, even among Israelites." Then he told the messengers to return to the pagan centurion who had seen, however dimly, that physical contact is not essential, since healing power derives from the Creator. Jesus sent him a direct assurance: "It will happen just as you believed it would." And he turned back toward the town.

Next day the district hummed with the news that the slave had recovered.

Despite the fact the miracle was performed after they begged Jesus to heed the centurion's request, the elders still barred him from the synagogue. The lakeshore became his pulpit. From cool early morning through the hot hours when Galileans normally sought shelter, and on into each evening, there seemed no end to the mass of ordinary folk from far and near who hungered to hear him. The Twelve and other disciples soaked up his words, while any casual traveler who stopped for an hour to listen would pass on the stories and sayings wherever he went, so that they spread from home to home, with excited accounts of how Jesus would interrupt his teaching to heal people. And this was happening in Galilee, despised by the orthodox and virtuous of Judea as a place of rough speech and bad habits, where too many Gentiles lived; a province of ignorance, compromise, and spiritual darkness.

Matthew summoned from his memory an apt reference from Isaiah about "Galilee of the Gentiles": " 'The people living in darkness,' " quoted Matthew, " 'have seen a great light; on those living in the shadow of death a light has dawned.' "

But Jesus' own family began to doubt his sanity. They had heard in Nazareth that he and his disciples neglected their meals because of the crowds; perhaps Salome herself told her sister, for Mary came down with his brothers to take him home for a rest. "He is out of his mind," they said. Mary wanted him to stop his work; his half brother James did not believe in him at all. They arrived one evening when he was back in Peter's house, still teaching the crowd in the courtyard.

The Nazareth family could not get through, like the paralyzed man's stretcher-bearers. Someone interrupted Jesus with a message. Jesus knew why Mary and James and the others had come, but he did not send the messenger back nor go out to meet them. Instead, he asked bluntly, "Who is truly my mother? Who are my real brothers? . . . They are here, sitting round me! Anyone who hears God's Word and does his will is my brother and my sister and my mother." He resumed teaching.

The implied rebuke, when conveyed to the family, hardened the opposition of James; much more would be needed before hostility turned to such devotion that he became the recognized leader of all in Jerusalem who called Jesus their Lord. But Mary quietly accepted it. Her mistaken mission had ended in a failure which she would never regret; the time came when she would leave home to help look after Jesus and his disciples on their travels, ensuring that they had enough to eat and time to eat it.

The incident emphasized the cost of following Jesus, especially to John and James, his cousins. They heard him say that if a man loved family "more than me," he was not worthy of him; that a man's foes would be those of his own household, that the choice might sometimes be so stark that loyalty to Jesus could seem hatred of father and mother. John had no doubt now where loyalty lay, even if his mother had tried to hinder. Pharisees might slander Jesus as in league with the prince of demons; religious leaders might scoff at him as a glutton and a winebibber, the friend of publicans and sinners.

Let them slander and scoff. Jesus was his Master, to copy, to support in whatever he planned to make men and women better in their ways as well as in their bodies. He brought great happiness. He had begun to curb John's hot temper and bring out the love and affection which lay beneath; to develop his mind, so that the fisherman would one day be the teacher and writer who could grasp profound truths and convey them in simple words. And beyond gratefulness for the influence of Jesus was an overriding desire for his company.

Yet fresh incidents showed how little John really knew him. One night after Jesus had gone to bed, Peter suggested that the partners go fishing. Though Zebedee had continued his business with the hired hands, and Salome was generous, cash from a good catch would be welcome in both households; and Judas Iscariot, who had been entrusted with the money box of the Twelve, had been muttering.

The four partners slipped away to the shore and took the two smaller boats. Each pair rowed out in the darkness, raised sail, and began to trawl. After a while they pulled in their nets and found nothing. They tried every favorite inlet; they ventured into deep water; they changed from dragnet to casting net, and met nothing but bad luck throughout the short summer night. Not a salable fish came into either boat. Peter grew so exasperated that he scared away any last hope of a catch by shouting inquiries to John and James. This made them angry. The nickname that Jesus had given them, Sons of Thunder, was thoroughly appropriate.

The four partners returned to shore at dawn in a bad temper. Boats seemed heavier to push from the water, and nets were more tangled and weedy than they could ever remember. And then came the first of the crowd, back at a favorite spot in the hope of hearing Jesus. Peter pretended not to notice. He gloomily continued to wash his net: Jesus could get the people in order himself and do his preaching.

At sunrise came Jesus. Out of the corner of an eye, Peter could see that he looked tired. The crowd pressed on him as he stood on the beach and began to talk about God. Peter paid closer attention to the washing of the nets.

The crowd grew, pushing those in front; Jesus stepped back and his feet were in the water. Suddenly he turned, took a few steps and leaped nimbly into Simon Peter's boat.

"Simon," he called, and when Peter looked up from his nets at hearing the old name rather than the new, he saw a hint of a twinkle in the eye, as if Jesus knew what was passing in his mind. "Simon, put out a little from the shore, please."

Peter climbed in, took up the oars and rowed a few strokes. Jesus sat on a thwart and resumed his teaching, his voice carrying all the more because of the few yards of water between speaker and audience. And he had the gift of making each man, woman, and child in a crowd feel that the words came intimately to himself or herself.

When the sun had risen high from behind the hills of the eastern shore, Jesus stopped; many of his hearers had work to do and families to support. Yet many lingered until they realized that Jesus would say no more that morning. They then dispersed.

Jesus turned to Peter and Andrew. "Put out into deep water and let down your nets for a catch."

Peter replied, "Master, we worked hard all night and caught nothing." He sounded a bit annoyed at the suggestion, half ashamed by his earlier behavior. Then he added, "But since it is you who tell us, I will."

Peter pulled the nets into the boat. John and James splashed across to their own boat and pushed her afloat. Both partners rowed their vessels out into the lake, steering courses about a quarter of a mile apart. When they reached deep water, Peter threw out his dragnets. Before John could throw out his, he heard a cry. Peter's boat appeared to be swaying violently, and he was pulling in already, struggling with a huge haul, which here and there broke the net; fish were falling back into the water. Peter shouted to the men in the other boat, and they rowed across to take some of the weight. The boats began to fill with struggling fish until the water was almost over the gunwales. John and James had never seen such a catch. Peter and Andrew, sweat pouring from their bodies, looked equally astounded, while Jesus sat apart on a thwart, since no fisherman wants a landsman to interfere.

Suddenly Peter dropped the fish he was handling. He turned and threw himself down at Jesus' knees in a gesture of total submission. His enormous frame was trembling. "Go away from me," he cried, "for I am a man who is a sinner, Lord."

"Don't be afraid," replied Jesus. "From now on you will catch men."

John heard. He shared Peter's feelings, though his own cry as a sinner might have been, "Stay close all the time! Never leave me, Lord." Jesus had repaid their petulance by giving them the catch of the season, which would be the talk of the lakeside for years. And he had awed them by an affinity with nature far beyond their professional skill.

They reached land, heaved their boats on shore, handed the catch to Zebedee and his men, and vowed never to desert Jesus again.

Seven
"WHO CAN HE BE?"

Jesus was teaching from the boat. This time, when the early morning crowds pressed near him, he told them a story.

The fields behind had now been harvested and the earth was hard. Jesus took his hearers forward to the familiar scene when the autumn rains would have softened the soil, and each farmer went out with his bag of seed to scatter it, handful by handful, as he walked carefully up and down. Only when he had sown his whole field, including the path which the villagers had trodden across the stubble, and the hidden rocks, and the soil which weeds had invisibly seeded, would he yoke his oxen and plow it in; this was the immemorial way in Palestine, sowing before plowing. Jesus took the plowing for granted in his hearers' minds.

"Listen carefully," he said. "A sower went out to sow. In his sowing, some fell on the path and the birds came and ate it. Some fell on the rocky places. Here the soil was thin and it sprang up quickly because it had little depth; when the sun came up the shoots were scorched, and withered away because they had no root.

"Other seed fell where the thorns were, and they grew up too and choked the shoots, and they never bore grain. And other seed fell into good soil and came up and grew and yielded a crop, increasing itself thirty, sixty, even a hundred times"—a harvest which evoked gasps of surprise from the listeners. Then Jesus rounded off his story with a challenge to solve its meaning: "Anyone who has ears, let him hear!"

The parable defeated all who heard it, whether those sitting or standing on the beach or those beside him in the boat. When the crowd dispersed to their daily work, Peter and John and some who remained on the shore begged for the key to the story. They also asked why he spoke in parables.

Jesus explained that he taught the horde of casual hearers by stories, and most of them would not understand the point: the meanings would remain hidden to any who did not genuinely want to know, for fear of having to turn from their old ways.

Those close to him, however, would be let into the secrets of God's kingdom. "Your eyes are happy and blessed because you really do see, and your ears because you really do hear. I tell you, and this is the truth: Many prophets and good men longed to see what you see but did not see it; and to hear what you hear and did not hear it."

Jesus gently suggested that the disciples should have seen for themselves the parable's points, and then he gave the explanation which would become so famous.

"The farmer sows the word," said Jesus. "The seed on the path is like those who hear the Word but do not understand,

and the evil one snatches it away at once. The seed sown on rocky land is the man who hears the Word and receives it with joy; but he has no root and lasts only a short time— when trouble or persecution comes on him because of the Word, he gives up.

"The seed among the thorns stands for those who hear, but the worries and pleasure of life and the deceitfulness of riches choke the Word, so that it never ripens. But the seed in the good soil stands for those who hear and accept and understand the Word and produce a fine crop—thirty, sixty, or a hundred times more than the farmer sowed."

That day Jesus gave all his teaching by parables, as people came and went, and whenever he was alone with the disciples he explained the meanings.

By nightfall he was exhausted. Instead of going home, he told the Twelve that he would accompany them to the other side of the lake, a sail of some six miles. Peter and John prepared one of the larger vessels. As they boarded, John inserted the detachable rudder oar and stood ready to steer, and Jesus went to the cushion beside it, lay down, and fell fast asleep. His face immediately lost its lines, as John saw by the light of the stern lamp; Jesus lay as peaceful as a child.

The fishermen among the Twelve took the oars and rowed the first half mile, then Peter hoisted sail to catch a gentle offshore breeze. The night was overcast, but they could steer toward the faint lights of the eastern shore. The first hour passed uneventfully as they sailed into the center of the lake. Suddenly, however, the wind rose. A squall swept without warning out of the lower Jordan Valley. Peter pulled in the sail to ride out the storm, and John, exerting his strength on the tiller, was amused by the slight panic of the landlubbers like Iscariot, and Simon, the former Zealot or freedom fighter. A sudden violent squall was common on the Sea of Galilee, locked below its mountains.

A few minutes later fear gripped John himself. He had never known such a storm. The sea raged, the rain cascaded, the ship tossed like a cork, while wave after wave broke over them, soaking them to the skin and filling the bilge. John secured the useless tiller and joined the others. As fast as they bailed, the water rose faster, and since a storm was always followed by a heavy swell lasting several hours, which would prevent them making land, John's experience warned him of disaster. They might founder—a frequent fate of ships in ancient times. A few more buffetings by huge waves, and the timbers would start, and all their bailing be useless.

The storm showed no sign of abating. The wind displayed a ferocity which even to a sailor like John seemed malevolent and personal, as if some supernatural force had designed their destruction.

In their panic no one had remembered Jesus. Several then struggled to the stern. They were astonished to see him lying there wet, but fast asleep, as if in bed ashore on the quietest summer night. They shook him awake. "Master, Master, we're going to drown!"

Somebody shouted, "We are going to perish, for all you care!"

Jesus stood up. He faced into the wind, not even steadying himself by holding a rope or a timber. In the tone of voice he had used to the demon in the synagogue, he spoke sharply to the elements. "Quiet!" he commanded the wind. "Be still!" he ordered the waves.

For the next seconds the Twelve could hardly believe their senses. Wind and waves dropped instantly. Nothing could be heard except a gentle slosh from the water on board. The sailors among them were astounded that not even a swell remained of the storm. They were drifting in a calm.

Jesus turned to his bedraggled disciples all soaked to the skin. "Why were you frightened?" he asked. "Have you still no faith?"

He went back to sleep. They loosed the rudder and began to bail out, shaken and terrified by his power over nature. They asked each other: "Who can he be, that he gives orders to the wind and the waves, and they obey him?"

They had plenty of time to reflect. The great calm kept the sail useless, and they had to work the oars, as if in penance for their lack of faith, while Jesus finished his sleep. After rowing for half an hour or so, Peter handed over his oar to a landlubber and threw out a net to catch fish for breakfast. Dawn broke to find them blown off course by the storm. Jesus woke and told them to make for shore, where they could light a fire and broil fish.

Hills riddled with caves came down to the waterline. As the boat neared land, they could see on the slope a large herd of pigs kept by Gentiles; this was repulsive to the disciples; pigkeeping was forbidden to Jews. The swineherds had lit a fire and were cooking.

John steered toward a small bay with a narrow beach. Peter put the vessel close in and, with a short splash, ankle high, all of them stepped ashore. John wondered what Jesus intended to do after they had eaten.

Before he could ask, a horrible cry rent the early morning quiet. A huge naked man emerged from one of the nearby caves, which probably contained a tomb, and ran toward them down the slope, yelling and leaping over boulders. His hair was long and matted. He had cuts on his arms and legs and chest, and he held a sharp flint, whether to cut himself again or to attack them, they could not tell.

Jesus stood his ground. In a stern, powerful voice he shouted, "Come out of this man, evil spirit!"

The man ran on, straight at Jesus, then stopped dead; he threw himself to his knees, and in a voice to wake the dead, he yelled the ancient challenge: "What have I to do with you—Jesus, *Son of the Most High God?*"

Peter gripped John's arm. The creature knew Jesus' name; and he had addressed him in a way which none of them would yet dare use, whatever his private hopes and half-formed beliefs; and the man had challenged Jesus to battle. Naked, strong as Samson, he looked even more fearsome at close quarters, for an iron shackle from which a broken chain hung loose gripped each wrist; his ankles were bruised and raw, as if he had smashed and wrenched irons off them. The cuts on his powerful chest, the bloodstains, the tangled body hair, the staring eyes made him horrifying.

"What have I to do with you?" he yelled again.

Jesus, in a firm, even voice, said: "What is your name?"

In reply, though Jesus stood only a foot away, the madman screamed: "My name is Legion, because there are so many of us."

Two thousand devils were destroying this man and challenging Jesus. One leap and Jesus would be crushed under a powerful torso while the stone and the shackles on the wrists could beat out his brains. Jesus had defeated the wind and waves. He was now at the mercy of a maniac; the disciples recoiled at the sense of evil and conflict.

Peter, the strongest built, took a step forward. Jesus gestured to him to stand still.

Looking straight at the man, Jesus spoke in an unforgettable tone which blended authority and compassion.

"Legion," he commanded, "come out of the man!"

The upshot was surprising. Legion spoke again, a little quieter but high-pitched: "Swear to God that you will not torture me! Don't banish us." Again and again Legion uttered the curious plea not to be sent away. At last he said, "Send us to the pigs; let us enter the pigs." His voice had the peculiar pitch of a man possessed.

The great herd of pigs fed in the browned grassland a little above the bay while the swineherds gaped at Jesus below; they never would have dared to venture close to Legion, the madman who snapped his chains when captured.

"Let us go into the hogs," cried Legion.

Jesus said something. The herd began to move. Two thousand pigs ran toward the sea, raced over the low cliff some twenty feet high, where the deep water of the lake had encroached on the slope, and here they drowned. The swineherds fled.

The disciples stood, shaken. Never in their lives had they seen a more dramatic lesson of the value of a human being. They recalled how Jesus had said that each of them was of more value than many sparrows, and that not one sparrow fell to the ground without the Heavenly Father's knowledge. Jesus knew what he was doing; if he had ruined the owners of the pigs and destroyed the livelihood of the swineherds, he had saved the sanity of a man.

John could see that Legion (whatever his real name) was different already. He was looking at Jesus with a smile. Then suddenly he realized that he was naked, and showed acute embarrassment. Peter ran to the boat and pulled out a spare garment, still a little damp but it would dry in the sunshine. Legion put it on gratefully. He helped them gather sticks to make a fire. But villagers were hurrying down, alerted by the agonized tale of the swineherds as they ran toward the town, which lay out of sight in a fold of the higher hills. Before Jesus and the disciples—with Legion—could finish eating their fish, they saw a dust cloud on the path from the town, as a string of riders on donkeys trotted to the bay; soon the pig owner and his neighbors and the local councilmen arrived.

"Go away!" they cried to Jesus. "Please go away!" They did not seem angry or heartbroken at the loss of the pigs, but frightened, especially when they saw the once-naked un-tamable man, decently clad, sane, and sitting on the ground beside Jesus.

"Go away! Go away!" they begged Jesus. Jesus did not try persuasion: he never seemed to press himself if not wanted. He stood up, beckoned to the disciples and made for the boat.

Legion was distraught. He ran after Jesus. "I want to go too. Please let me be with you always."

He would have become an unusual companion, a Gentile disciple before the time, and needing patient understanding as he rebuilt his life, across the lake and far from home.

Jesus looked upon him compassionately and spoke gently, his voice a contrast from the stern, powerful tones he had used when Legion had first appeared. "No," he said. "You cannot come with me. Go home. Find your family and tell them how much the Lord has done for you. Tell them how he had mercy on you."

Legion smiled back at Jesus, with the thought of home and family and a story to tell which would amaze them. As Jesus sat down in the stern of the boat, the disciples rowed from shore, and Legion, in Peter's spare coat, stood waving, with his neighbors gathered around, until his great frame grew small and they could no longer see him.

Eight
"IT IS TIME TO WAKE UP!"

A gentle breeze off the eastern hills gave good progress, but the morning was now well advanced and the heat kept Capernaum hazy until the vessel neared the harbor with the sun right behind her. Then they saw a crowd on the shore, visible beyond the masts and hills of ships already berthed, and another on the beach from which they had sailed the night before.

Peter trimmed sail. John steered toward a vacant berth at the quay. The crowd surged toward them, and when Andrew threw a rope, willing hands made the vessel fast. John saw at once that this was no casual welcome, for as Jesus stepped onto shore, the crowd parted and Jairus, president of the synagogue, identified by the rich linen of his summer tunic before they recognized his features, ran forward from the bench where he had waited in the shade. John's nerves fluttered, for Jairus was powerful and his presence might mean trouble; but Jairus dropped on his knees in front of Jesus, and when he looked up, his face under his headdress was ravaged by worry and grief.

"My little daughter is dying," he cried. "Please, *please* come and put your hands on her so that she is healed and will live. Please, oh, please do this!"

The irony was rich. They had flung Jesus out of the synagogue, yet the elders had interceded for the pagan centurion; and now comes the president begging Jesus to heal his daughter.

Thoughts so unworthy were quickly killed by the distress of Jairus, and by Jesus' instant response. "I will come with you," he said. Jairus and Jesus set off together.

The people pressed behind and at their side, while more came running toward them. When they turned into a narrower street which took a shortcut toward the richer quarter, Peter and John and the others could hardly clear a path because everybody wanted to be nearest to Jesus. Suddenly he stopped and turned around.

"Who touched me?" he asked.

No one answered. He asked again. Peter replied, a trifle rudely, "Master, you can see they are all around and pushing you about. How can you possibly ask, 'Who touched me?' "

Jesus said, "Someone touched me. I know, because power went out from me."

He walked on slowly, looking around as if determined to find out who touched him.

Then a woman about thirty years old broke past John and fell on her knees. She trembled, yet wonder and joy, with a hint of fear, suffused her face as she poured out her story to Jesus. She came from a distant village, she said. For twelve years a continual flow of menstrual blood had rendered her ritually unclean, caused her to be shunned, and prevented a normal life. She had spent all her patrimony on doctors without success.

Hearing about Jesus, she came to Capernaum. She could not get near enough to plead with him. "But I said to myself," she told him, "that if I can just touch the fringe of his garment, I shall be well again. And I pushed my way nearer. And I touched. And I knew at that very moment that the blood had stopped and I was well! That's the whole truth!"

She seemed worried that he would tell her she had stolen her cure. Instead, he looked down at the woman kneeling before him, "Daughter,"—and his voice had a special tenderness—"your faith has healed you. Go in peace. You are free from your suffering."

Throughout their talk, Jairus had wrung his hands at the delay, and as if to justify his fears, he saw two or three of his friends elbowing their way down the street. They reached him while Jesus still comforted the woman. They spoke almost callously.

"Your daughter is dead," they said. "Why bother the teacher anymore?" There was contempt in their tone: he had healed the centurion's slave but this time had failed. They had disapproved of calling in the prophet of Nazareth.

Jesus put a hand on Jairus' arm and looked him straight in the eye. "Do not be afraid," he said. "Simply believe."

He beckoned to John, James, and Peter; not even Andrew was to come; he and the other eight must keep the people from following, and await his return.

Jairus led the way. Nearing Jairus' mansion, they heard women wailing and the sound of flutes; and entering the courtyard they saw that the professional mourners, with hair hanging down, had begun their dance of death. Wailing and clapping in rhythm to a lament played on the flutes, they moved slowly in a circle round their leader.

Jesus spoke sharply: "What is all this commotion and noise? The girl is not dead. She is asleep!" The mourners gave a loud cackle of laughter: each one of them had viewed the corpse. The grief-stricken mother, however, had come out of the death room on hearing Jesus' voice, and hope crossed her face as Jesus ordered the mourners and flutists to leave; his tone of quiet authority subdued them and sent them meekly into the street, leaving only relatives and close neighbors in the courtyard.

Jesus asked the parents to take him to their daughter's body and allowed no others except Peter, James, and John to enter the death chamber.

It seemed dark after the strong sunshine in the courtyard, but when their eyes adjusted to the shade, John saw the girl, who looked about twelve years old, lying on her bed in such peace that she might indeed have been asleep were it not for her pallor. The silent grief of the parents deepened the stillness. John felt that he and his brother and Peter were almost intruding, though grateful that their presence might support Jesus in whatever he had to do.

Jesus took her by the hand. A rather beautiful look crossed his face. Then he said what any mother or father would say to a girl when waking her up in the morning. *"Talitha koum! It's time to wake up, little girl!"*

The girl opened her eyes. She sat up and got off her bed. The parents clung to each other with amazement and joy and gratitude as she walked toward them and flung her arms wide in greeting.

Before they could thank him or fully take in what had happened, Jesus spoke briskly like a physician. "Give her something to eat!" Then, in contrast to his instruction that morning to Legion, he gave a strict order: "On no account tell anyone what happened"—an order which, in the excitement and relief soon to burst on the household and neighborhood, would be hard to obey.

Nine
A CONTRAST
IN COMPASSION

In the last weeks of summer, Jesus decided to take the Twelve into the hill country of Galilee. The days would be cooler, the crowds less, and he could train them for the future as they walked between the villages before they all went up to Jerusalem. Besides, the citizens of Capernaum and neighboring towns of the Sea of Galilee were behaving as if he had never come among them. They had brought him their sick, they had hung on his words, but most did not repent.

Before Jesus set out, he was summoned to dine with a Pharisee named Simon, one of those who had publicly disgraced him by banning his teaching in synagogues.

Such an invitation seemed strange until he crossed the threshold, with Peter and John, and found himself insulted. Simon pointedly refrained from giving him the kiss of welcome; no servant brought the usual bowl to wash street dust from his feet, and no drop of aromatic oil was sprinkled on his head.

Jesus appeared not to notice, though John thought he detected a twinkle in his eye as Jesus gravely joined the other guests already reclining at table. He was led to the couch beside his host, who at least had not put him at the lowest place, and ate what was brought and listened as Simon told him how he fasted twice a week, gave tithes of all he possessed, and was a most virtuous man.

Just then a woman came in from the courtyard holding a small jar. She stood behind Jesus as he lay on the couch and gazed at him. Though there was nothing unusual in a neighbor's watching a feast uninvited, Simon the Pharisee tensed. The woman was soberly dressed but she was lovely. As she gazed at Jesus, she began to weep. She knelt and allowed the tears to bathe his bare feet; then she shook her hair and began to dry his feet with her tresses and kiss them repeatedly. Undoubtedly, she was a woman of much experience with men, yet her actions were purged of suggestiveness. Her charms were so strong that John almost needed to remember a warning which Jesus had given, that a lustful look is equal to the act of adultery. But the woman was not making advances; plainly she had thrown her past behind her.

Suddenly she broke the neck of her little jar and poured its contents on Jesus' feet. Quickly a luscious scent filled the room. Whether the perfume had been given her by a lover or bought as an aid to her arts, she poured it with reverence.

Jesus had not moved, except to gaze back at her in a compassion and a love which neither condemned nor recoiled. Simon, on the other hand, bridled with distaste. His sneer disclosed his thoughts: that this man was no prophet or he would have detected a prostitute at once.

Jesus turned to him. "Simon," he said, "I want to tell you something."

"What is it, Teacher?"

"There was a moneylender with two debtors. One owed him five hundred, the other fifty. Neither had anything with which to pay him. So he canceled the debts of both. Which of them will love him more?"

"I suppose," replied Simon in a rather grudging tone, "the one who had the bigger debt canceled."

"You are right. Now, listen." Then Jesus publicly contrasted Simon's lapses in hospitality with what the woman had done: it was she who had washed his feet, who had given him kisses and anointed him. "Therefore, I tell you, her sins have been forgiven, for she loved much. Someone who has been forgiven little, loves little."

He looked with compassion at the woman. "Your sins have been forgiven."

Guests muttered angrily, "Who does he think he is, forgiving sins?"

Jesus ignored their mutterings. "Your faith has saved you," he said to the woman. "Go in peace."

Next day, John walked into the hills with Jesus and the others. As they went from village to village, Jesus showed his marvelous gift for speaking so that poor and rich, simple and wise, could understand him. He had acute powers of observation, as his parables showed. Naturally, he knew about carpentry and building; equally, he could make his points with stories about sheep and wheat farming, about vineyards and fig trees and pigs. He had a shrewd idea of trade and business so that he could tell of bad and good stewards, and moneylenders and tax men; he had observed the ways of the wealthy and of those so poor that a lost coin made a matter of utmost concern; he could describe scribes in flowing robes, judges and kings; burglars operating at night and highway robbers. Using word pictures and pithy comments, he could make truth plain, bring all heaven before the inward eyes of his hearers, and probe the ways of man.

He showed a compassion which came from the roots of his soul. He grieved to see men and women helpless and drifting and oppressed. His instinct was to bring immediate comfort and relief.

An unexpected incident near a town called Nain brought this out vividly. Followed by the inescapable crowd from villages recently visited, Jesus and his disciples approached the town gateway just as an equally large crowd left it. In the center four men carried a corpse. They were weeping, and beside them a woman wept even more. The two crowds met. When Jesus saw the woman, a spasm of pain crossed his face and he said, "Don't cry!"

He turned around and walked with her. Townsfolk explained that she was a widow; the corpse was of her only son and support, and they had been devoted to each other. He had died that morning. Burials always took place the same day, but she could not bear to see him go and had refused to allow them to wrap his face before they reached the graveside. Almost all the town came with her in sympathy.

Jesus stepped across to the bier. Those carrying it stopped. He said, "Young man, I say to you: *get up!*"

At once the man sat up and began to talk. Jesus turned to the mother and smiled. With a gesture that suggested the return of a prisoner-of-war or of someone ransomed from slavery, he formally handed the young man back to his mother.

A few weeks earlier Jesus had raised from the dead the daughter of Jairus, ruler of the Capernaum synagogue. John, James, and Peter had looked on, amazed. That had been in the privacy of a darkened room. At Nain they were in the open, and the people were awestruck. They did not shout nor laugh for joy; they stood and sang a psalm of praise. The town's patriarch voiced their feelings: "A great prophet has arisen among us." And a younger man echoed, "God has visited his people."

John, Peter, and the other disciples echoed those words too. But though Jesus spoke often of "the kingdom," he had not yet made plain whether he would create this kingdom soon and throw out the Romans by mobilizing his vast following or by supernatural aid; nor whether the kingdom lay far in the future. He spoke to his disciples as if the history of their race would reach its climax in himself. Sometimes he seemed indeed the Messiah foretold in ancient times, who would judge and purge; at other times he seemed perplexingly different, so gentle and willing to suffer.

The answers had eluded John. Then, in the next months from autumn through to spring, several events threw a flood of light; and the twelve months after that would show the truth to be far more terrible and glorious than anything John had imagined.

Ten
NO GOING BACK

After he had preached outside a town in the Galilean hills, large crowds pressed around Jesus. People brought him their sick, those who were lame, and others in distress. The Twelve worked, as always, to keep patients and suppliants in some sort of order.

In the midst of it, John noticed two travel-stained men whose rough clothes and ascetic faces set them apart as disciples of John the Baptist. At once he stopped what he was doing and asked for news of his old master, who languished in a dungeon in Herod's grim fortress of Machaerus in the wild country beyond the Dead Sea. The messengers said that Herod, when in residence, would question him and listen, and seemed in awe of him, but would not release him or put him on trial.

The men were in no mood for talk. They said they must

speak urgently to Jesus, for their master had heard of his doings and wanted to ask a question. John maneuvered them through the importunate crowd until they reached him.

"Sir," they said, "John the Baptist has sent us to ask you if you are the 'Coming One'? Or should we look for someone else?"

If Jesus felt a pang of regret at the Baptist's doubts, he did not show it. Nor did he reply. Disciples of the Baptist had once asked why he did not fast or refuse wine or strong drink, and he had answered that no one wept or fasted in a bridegroom's presence, though they would when he was removed.

This time he went silently back to his work, so that as the Baptist's messengers watched, blind people saw again and the lame walked; others in the grip of madness or epilepsy or evil spirits became their normal selves; even lepers who had dared to mingle in the crowd were restored: it is sometimes forgotten that Jesus healed hundreds of sufferers whose stories were not recorded and would have healed more had they sought him.

Jesus gave the messengers time to gather evidence with their own eyes and from witnesses of earlier incidents. Then he told them to return and report, and to quote to the Baptist a passage from Isaiah's prophecy of what would happen when the Messiah came: "The blind receive their sight, the lame walk, lepers are cleansed, and the deaf hear; the dead are raised up, and the poor have Good News preached to them." Jesus added, "Happy is the man who has no doubts about me."

As the messengers left, Jesus praised John the Baptist as a prophet, and more than a prophet because he was the herald who had made men ready for the king. None greater than John had ever been born; "yet," Jesus told them, "he who is least in the kingdom of heaven is greater than he." The crowd, who listened intently as they sat or stood on the sunbaked earth, were left in no doubt that a new era had begun.

In a long sermon that afternoon, Jesus spoke of his sorrow that Capernaum and the cities on the lake, with their Pharisees and scribes, religious and learned, had not turned from their sins; if his miracles had been done in Gentile cities, or even in ancient Sodom, which was a byword for wickedness, the citizens would have repented and escaped judgment. At one point Jesus looked around at his humble audience of simple country folk and lifted his hands in prayer. "I praise You, Father, Lord of heaven and earth, because you have hidden these things from the wise and prudent and revealed them to little children."

Then came the climax of Jesus' sermon which would be quoted and pondered on and loved by humanity through all the ages to come. His eye had caught an ox cart, drawn by two yoked oxen; the driver had stopped and sat listening. One of the oxen was young, the other strong and experienced. The load was heavy, but everybody knew that when they moved again the young ox would find that the older took the strain and showed the way.

"Come to me," cried Jesus, "all you who are weary and burdened, and I will give you rest. Take my yoke upon you and learn of me, for I am gentle and humble in heart, and you will find rest to your souls. For my yoke is easy and my burden is light"—immortal words which, to John and those who knew him well, expressed the very heart of the man.

Soon afterward, Jesus took the disciples to Jerusalem for one of the great festivals. As was his way, he sought out the distressed. He went on the Sabbath to the Pool of Bethesda (or Bezatha), an ancient reservoir or tank with five porticoes,

outside the city walls near the sheep gate. Because its water
bubbled at intervals, Bethesda attracted the lame, the blind,
and the sick in the belief that the first to enter after the water
bubbled would be cured. Therefore, most were escorted by
friends or relatives ready to act.

Jesus was unknown by sight. He walked in the porticoes
and no one sought his aid. Suddenly the water bubbled.
Uproar followed as escorts fought to get their patients into
the pool. Jesus noticed an emaciated man of late middle age
trying desperately by crawls and jerks to reach the water
unaided, and then dragging himself sadly back to his pallet.
Jesus approached him. The man had been an invalid for
thirty-eight years, though John in relating the incident did
not record how long he had waited at the pool.

"Do you want to get well?" asked Jesus.

The man answered in despair, "I have no one to help me
into the pool when the water bubbles. While I am trying,
someone always gets in first."

"Get up! Pick up your pallet! Walk!"

The man had neither sought aid nor shown faith; but he
responded to the stranger's command at once. At the first
movement, all weakness or paralysis disappeared. He redis-
covered his strength, picked up his pallet, and walked away
from the pool without a word of thanks.

None of the sick or escorts noticed, too intent on waiting
for the next bubble in the pool. Jesus quickly left, followed
by John and Peter. As they went down the street, John saw
the man and his pallet out of the corner of his eye; he had
been stopped by Pharisees, who were pointing at the pallet
he carried on a Sabbath Day.

An hour or so later they met the man again, in the precincts of the Temple; perhaps he had come to offer thanks
for his healing. Jesus knew that the illness of thirty-eight

years had been the sufferer's fault, possibly as a consequence of fornication, and he warned him to cease sinning or worse might happen. The man did not take the warning kindly; he hurried away and shortly afterward a posse of Pharisees descended on Jesus to accuse him of incitement to Sabbath breaking: they had stopped someone carrying a pallet, they said, and he had now pointed out the person who had caused him to pick it up. Some of the accusers had been among the investigators in Galilee who had seen Jesus restore the withered hand in the synagogue on a Sabbath.

They immediately put him on trial, informally, in the Temple precincts, under one of the porches where debates were held. This debate might lead to formal arraignment: once again Jesus stood under the shadow of death, by judicial process or by murder in a back street.

John stood beside Jesus and marveled at his courage as he took up the challenge. His accusers demanded to know why he worked on the Sabbath. He answered by words which made them certain that he claimed to be equal with God, whom he called "my Father," an expression no Jew would dare to use. Not denying their interpretation, Jesus emphasized his relationship with God until no one present remained in doubt of his claim that his life and actions revealed the life and action of God. He claimed that he had power to give men life and that he, Jesus, would be their judge. He asserted that men should honor him exactly as they honored the Father. With strong emphasis, Jesus said, "Whoever hears my word and believes him who has sent me has eternal life and will not be condemned; he has crossed over from death to life."

His claims were uncompromising, forceful, and put him beyond retreat, being blasphemous delusion or fraud unless true. And since a man's testimony about himself was not valid, he cited as evidence John the Baptist's statements about him, and the witness of the miracles of healing and life which no human being had ever achieved before. The Father himself, he said, had spoken in witness, though the accusers had never heard his voice nor seen his shape.

He went on: "You search the Scriptures because you think that in them you have eternal life. They bear witness to *me!*" cried Jesus. Suddenly his eyes filled with compassion for his accusers in their emptiness and blindness. "They bear witness to me, yet you refuse to come to me to have life!

"I do not accept man's praise," he said. "But I know you. You do not have God's love in your hearts. I have come in my Father's name and you reject me, yet if someone comes in his own name you will accept him. You accept praise from each other but do not try to obtain the praise that comes from the Only One."

By now he had turned the tables. "Do not think I will accuse you to the Father! Your accuser is Moses, on whom your hopes are set. If you believed Moses, you would believe me, for he wrote about me. But since you do not believe what he wrote, how are you going to believe what I say?"

They had no answer. They let him go. But he had signed his death warrant, however long it took to execute.

Eleven
TO MAKE HIM
A KING

Jesus took his disciples back to Galilee. They did not go by way of Samaria, which Jews avoided when traveling at festival times, but down to the coast and then northward up the Great South Road built by the Romans. They turned with it into the hills. Jesus was heading for Nazareth, which he had not visited since his rejection and escape from murder before he had called John and the others from their fishing.

Throughout the journey, John walked under the spell of Jesus' answer to the Jewish leaders who had arraigned him, the speech in which he had stated his claims with authority, yet without histrionics or rhetoric. Yet neither John nor Peter nor any of them could force their lips to make open acknowledgment that this man who walked beside them, so like themselves though so different, was the Son of God.

They left the Great Road near Sepporis and climbed the

few miles to Nazareth on a wet day of autumn rain and mist, to be welcomed by Mary without restraint. The formidable half brother, James, was more cautious, and the rest of the family still hardly knew what to make of the extraordinary events and stories which had surrounded Jesus for the past twenty months. On the Sabbath they all went to the synagogue. The ban of the Capernaum elders did not run elsewhere, and Jesus was invited to teach.

The townsfolk proved even less responsive than before. "Isn't this the carpenter's son?" they sneered, seeing him only as the local lad of earlier memories, whose relations were their neighbors. They had nothing against him, could recall no sowing of wild oats; indeed, they remembered his youth with affection and admiration. But they would not go further. Thus, the people of Nazareth dashed any hope that they would help him take his message to the surrounding countryside, or later would cross the seas on his behalf. Talking with his disciples in the privacy of Mary's home, he expressed amazement at Nazareth's refusal to believe in him, and his pain that their lack of faith frustrated his desire to help them. A blind man or two and a few sick sought him out and were healed, but Nazareth as a town turned its back on the one who would give them their only place in world history. John summed it up later in the matchless prologue to his Gospel, with a wider context: "He came to his own and his own did not receive him."

Rejected at Capernaum, Jerusalem, and Nazareth, he still had the Twelve. They might not fully understand, but they trusted him and he could trust them; when he led them away from his home to visit local villages, he disclosed that he would soon send them out on their own. Winter was coming on, when the crowds would not want to gather in the cold winds and the rain and hail or snow. This would be the season for smaller meetings.

First, Jesus trained them. He taught them what to do and to expect, both in the immediate short term and during the long years to come, when they would be hauled before kings and governors for his sake, be beaten in the synagogues, be forced to flee from one city to another. "Don't be afraid," he told them; and again, "I am sending you out as sheep in the midst of wolves. Be wise as serpents and innocent as doves." What he had told them in secret they were to proclaim from the housetops.

They went out in pairs, John with James, Peter with Andrew, and the others paired as seemed best. Carrying out his instructions, they took no stick, no spare coat, nor money in their belts. When they reached a town or village, they asked residents for lodging; they accepted hospitality without offering any return except the privilege of aiding their work; but they refused to accept handouts of money, not even a penny. They avoided Gentile towns, nor did they enter Samaria, but went among the villages of their own Jewish people, and preached Jesus' message: "The kingdom of heaven is at hand." In some places they were rebuffed, and then, as Jesus had instructed, they turned their backs and at the town's edge, formally removed a shoe, and shook off the dust.

Jesus had said, "Heal the sick, raise the dead, cleanse the lepers, cast out demons." Not one disciple had ever done such things, though they had watched him often enough. John, conscious that away from Jesus he was nothing but a fisherman who had left his nets, went to it nervously. To his utter astonishment, when he placed his hands on the first sick person, he was at once aware of extraordinary power, as if Jesus himself stood by.

Jesus had told the Twelve where to meet him when the

winter ended. But when the day came for reunion, and John and James took the last turn to join the trail to the rendezvous, with a glimpse of Peter and Andrew marching steadily uphill half a mile in front, the whole countryside was in a ferment because of news from beyond the Jordan: Herod had beheaded the Baptist.

Jesus, they soon found, had already received details of the squalid events which had led to the execution. Herod, though a Jew, had celebrated his birthday at the fortress of Machaerus in a pagan manner, by a great banquet for his army chiefs, local governors, and all the high and mighty of the tetrarchy. His wife, Herodias, knew that the Baptist was chained in a cell below the banqueting hall. She loathed him for his courage in rebuking them when Herod had seduced her from his own half brother, Philip, and had long sought an occasion to destroy him. She now sent her daughter by Philip to dance before a tipsy stepfather and his guests. Salome danced in such a way that Herod promised on oath to give her anything she wanted. Her mother had told her already what to ask: "the head of John the Baptist on a dish." Herod was horrified, but a perverted sense of honor held his oath more sacred than natural justice or his admiration for John. And so, the great voice had been silenced by the heavy short sword of a guard. John the Baptist, the powerful moral influence, "the burning and shining light," was gone.

The people of Judea and Galilee were shocked and angry: the Baptist had been a voice of national resurgence. For Jesus, and for John and Peter, the Baptist's death was a deep personal sorrow.

There was no time for weeping or fond remembrance: the stirring throughout the nation had come at the same time as a stirring in Galilee caused by their own mission; before the disciples could give Jesus all their news as they walked together toward Capernaum, he was again the center of demanding crowds, coming and going, who made no secret of their conviction that Jesus was worth more than all his Twelve together. The following days were filled from morning to night, with time for only the most hurried of informal meals, or none.

Jesus was determined to give his Twelve a brief recess, when they could talk over with him their experiences and lessons in a restful, reinvigorating way. Early one morning before the town was astir, they all crept to the shore, enjoying the conspiratorial way in which Jesus gave the crowd the slip. They embarked in Peter's boat.

Rain had fallen for much of the night; Passover was only ten days away and the intermittent spring rains had come. The mist rose from the water, though the day looked as if it would turn fine. Jesus sat in the stern at the tiller, and since the wind had dropped, all the Twelve took oars; landlubbers like Judas Iscariot had now learned the knack. Jesus had suggested they should go across the top of the lake, beyond Bethsaida Julius, to a rather desolate area where the land rose in steep green folds from the shoreline. Thus, they would not be spotted by people in the villages higher up; and many of these would be Gentiles who would not care.

Jesus did not want to make a straight course; by spending part of the morning on the lake, they could rest and be fresh upon reaching land. Thus, they passed close to the quay at Capernaum as they set out. None of them at the oars noticed a man staring at the boat; nor did they realize that he had recognized the profile of Jesus before the boat disappeared into the mist; least of all did they know the wild surmise that passed through this man's mind, and that he was rushing to spread the news of Jesus' arrival in the area.

The lake in the early morning refreshed them as the sun broke through the mist. Fishing vessels had put into shore after the night's work, and the carriers of merchandise and men had not come out; Jesus and his disciples had the Sea of Galilee to themselves. More than once they put up the oars and drifted while one after another put questions to Jesus or told him of encouraging or perplexing incidents. Sometimes they rocked with laughter at some memory; it was easy to be happy with Jesus. Then someone would recall a memory of the Baptist, and their great sorrow would come to the forefront and they wept; neither tears nor laughter seemed out of place in Jesus' company.

The sun grew strong. It was time to continue their day of rest in shade on a hillside. They rowed again, for the wind was offshore.

Their backs were toward the land and it was not until they reached shallow water and heard a great cheer behind them that the Twelve realized what Jesus in the stern had seen already. A huge crowd awaited him in the isolated place where they had expected to relax. The disciples turned on their thwarts in disgust and disappointment. Not only was the beach crowded, but they could see hundreds of men running toward the lake from the direction of Bethsaida; and had the disciples been high up instead of on the water, they would have seen that the road which led over the Jordan ford from Capernaum and Magdala and Tiberias was thick with men running.

John felt a spasm of anger that Jesus, who had seen the crowd, had not directed the boat to another beach; but once again this unworthy thought died when he turned and saw the compassion on Jesus' face. He also saw a slight hardening of the jaw, and as they stowed oars and jumped into the shallow water to pull the vessel on to the beach, he realized why Jesus' countenance had suddenly changed. This was no ordinary crowd. It was mostly male. Women and children, with their sick, had followed, but most of those who had run round the lake to meet Jesus were men and some were armed. They were not intending harm against Jesus: the mood was of excitement, of a desire for leadership, of a mass movement like a flock of sheep which would race wherever the bellwether went, if the shepherd were not there to control. The glint of the sun on steel suggested that some of the men hoped that Jesus would lead them at once to avenge the Baptist.

Jesus stood for a few moments surveying the scene. Then he walked at a steady pace inland, the men making way, and climbed to a little rise which formed a convenient pulpit to the natural amphitheater sloping down to the beach. The great crowd stood or sat noisily below him.

First, he ordered that any sick should be brought; he healed them, and this amazed and quieted the people. Then, with a gesture for total silence, he began to preach. With the land breeze carrying his voice, the people listened unwearied, hour by hour; it seemed that all thought of violence was stilled and that they would indeed "seek first the kingdom of God and his righteousness."

When the sun had moved into the west, Jesus stopped preaching. The crowd of several thousand were now very hungry. Some of the disciples suggested that he send the people into the surrounding villages to buy themselves food; but since they were in a desolate spot, where the few villages higher up could supply little, and since darkness would fall before anyone could reach the larger towns, this was a callous policy to urge.

Jesus rejected it. "You give them something to eat," he said, and John noticed again the twinkle in his eye, and was sure he wanted to test them.

Philip fell into the trap. "Two hundred *denarii*—eight months' wages—would not buy enough bread for everyone to have a bite. Are we to spend that amount?"

"How many loaves have you got here? Go and see."

The Twelve scattered to discover provisions among the vast number of people present, estimated at 5,000 men, plus women and children. But any who had hurriedly made up bags of food at the sudden rush after Jesus had long since eaten what they carried. John, Peter, Philip, and eight others found nothing. Andrew, however, met a small boy whom he probably knew, for the boy likely came from Bethsaida. The boy evidently had been on his way to bring supper to his father and brother keeping sheep on the hillside, and had been caught up in the crowd and had stayed to listen.

Andrew hurried to Jesus. "Here is a lad with five little barley loaves and two small dried fish—but what are they among so many?"

With a smile of thanks, Jesus took the loaves and fishes from the boy. Coarse barley bread was food for the poorest: three loaves, helped down by tasty morsels of dried fish, made one adult's meal, but Jesus had more than 5,000 to feed. Before the disciples could wonder what he intended, he ordered them to seat the crowd, many of whom had begun to wander around restlessly. Significantly, the people formed themselves into companies of fifties or hundreds, as if a military chain of command had been at work.

They all waited expectantly. Jesus held in his hands the five loaves and two little fish and looked up to heaven. He gave thanks as if he were the head of a household presiding at a feast. Then he broke up the five loaves. He handed broken bread to each of the Twelve, and pieces of the two dried fish, and ordered them to distribute the pieces among

5,000 hungry men, with their women and children.

Feeling a fool, but obeying Jesus without question, John walked toward a company of fifty or a hundred holding less than half a loaf and one sixth of a little fish. In a gesture of faith, he tore a generous lump from his half loaf, and a piece of fish, and handed the food to the first man in the first rank. When John looked down to see how to divide the remainder, he saw half a loaf still in his hand, and the portion of fish apparently undiminished. When he had fed the second man, he saw the same. With mounting excitement, he went down the line, tearing off larger portions. Thoughts raced through his mind of the wine at Cana of Galilee, and of Elijah's flour and oil which never failed in the famine long ago, as they often heard in synagogue; but Elijah had fed only himself and a small family, and Jesus at Cana had supplied a mere village wedding, whereas on this spring evening above the lakeshore, Jesus was feeding more than 5,000.

By now John and his friends were handing out almost all of a half loaf, and men were passing the pieces of bread down the line; still the supply did not fail.

No one went hungry. Before this extraordinary feast was over, many were taking more than they could eat, so that fragments were thrown on the ground. As John worked, power seemed to flow through his hands, and his heart leaped with the sheer joy of being part of this incredible creation; never had he felt closer to Jesus, although separated by rank upon rank of amazed and excited Galileans.

At last, at Jesus' order, the disciples gathered up all that was left on the ground, stacking twelve baskets in front of him. It was now almost dark, but the excitement of the people could scarcely be contained. Some were already drawing their swords, demanding that Jesus accept the throne usurped by Herod, and lead them at once, through the night, on a march of vengeance to overthrow Herod and his Roman overlords.

John felt himself beginning to be swept into a mass movement. When he looked at Judas Iscariot and at Simon the former Zealot, he could see the light of battle in their eyes. Then Jesus made a most unexpected move. He ordered the Twelve to return to the boat and to sail or row back to Capernaum; he would dismiss the crowd himself.

Such was his authority that they obeyed. Fears for his safety, regrets that he could not trust them, were extinguished. While the crowd watched, they walked meekly down to the shore. They heard afterward that Jesus had ordered the leaders of the incipient revolt to disperse their followers and that most had started back along the shore by the light of a nearly full moon while some had settled down where they were. Jesus had disappeared; he had been last seen climbing into the hills, and no one had dared to follow or to dispute his refusal to be made a king.

Meanwhile the Twelve had put out to sea. They hung about offshore for several hours, rowing up and down because they expected Jesus to signal to them that he wanted to come on board. About midnight they gave up and set course for the opposite shore. The breeze which had blown from the west during the afternoon had veered and they had to row without help of the sail. The farther they progressed toward the center of the lake, the more the wind stiffened and the waves buffeted the boat. The long day and its excitement and the lateness of the hour had sapped their strength, until even the hardiest sailor was in distress as he strained at his oar. Their memory of a miracle was washed out by the misery of backbreaking toil, though they faced the distant shore, still clear in the moonlight, where they had distributed the loaves and fish.

Suddenly one of them gave a cry. Then they all cried out in fear. Between them and the shore they saw a man walking on the water toward them, moving quickly despite the waves but on a parallel course. The apparition looked like Jesus. Terrified, they were certain that it was his ghost; he must have been killed by the mob: they should have ignored his command and stayed to save him.

The figure neared the boat. They cried out again.

Suddenly they heard Jesus' unmistakable voice above the wind and the waves. "Be brave," he shouted. "It is I! Don't be afraid!"

Peter apparently thought Jesus was going to pass them by. Impulsive as always, he yelled, "Lord, if it is you, tell me to come to you on the water!"

"Come!"

Peter, the experienced fisherman, who knew that the fresh-water lake lacked even the partial buoyancy of the Dead Sea, left the boat. Amazed, the other disciples saw Peter walk toward Jesus. Then suddenly Peter lost his nerve. He began to sink, and they heard a despairing cry, "Lord, save me!"

Jesus stretched out his hand and gripped Peter. " 'Little-Faith,' why did you doubt?" they heard him say. The two were close to the vessel. Willing hands helped them and, as they climbed aboard, the wind dropped.

John, Peter, and the others were utterly astonished that Jesus should have reached them. They could no more understand how he walked on water than how he multiplied loaves and fish. They gaped at him.

Then one after another stumbled over the oars to fall at his feet. "You are the Son of God," they cried. "It is true! It is utterly true—you are the Son of God!"

But they hardly knew what they said.

Part Two
DEATH IN JERUSALEM

Twelve
THE MOUNTAIN

The great road Via Maris (Way of the Sea) bore a steady two-way traffic of camel caravans and donkey trains, of military detachments marching in the dust, of slaves and prisoners and strings of horses being led for sale. This was the road which Saul of Tarsus traveled a few years later on his way to Damascus, breathing threats and slaughter against disciples of Jesus: a journey which had an unexpected end.

In the high summer of A.D. 29, Jesus and the Twelve and a few other followers walked north on Via Maris. They could see the Golan Heights on their right and Mount Hermon far ahead, still with snow wedged below the summit despite the summer sun. Its coolness beckoned them from the heat which hung round the Sea of Galilee.

At the Ford of Jacob's Daughters, where Via Maris crosses the Jordan, Jesus turned off the Damascus Road onto a quieter route of Upper Galilee. They walked on, mile after mile, at a steady pace, through a city and round the western shores of the small lake into which the young Jordan flows after threading its way through the marshes.

When they were well into the hills, Jesus left the main road and they climbed upward. If anyone grew tired after traveling through the heat of the day, Jesus insisted on carrying his burden, though Peter tried to stop him and take it himself. The track became steep, but Jesus pressed on and upward until at length, as darkness fell, they reached the spot where one of the sources of the Jordan gushes out of the rock face, which the Greeks called the Springs of Pan, after the god of shepherds.

They slept where they were, for the summer night was warm even at that height. At dawn, as they woke, a pagan shepherd came up to the Springs of Pan and threw in a votive offering. When the sun rose, they saw in the distance the magnificent sight of the city of Caesarea Philippi, which Herod the Great had built and Philip the Tetrarch had expanded to make his capital; its newness was almost dazzling. High above stood Mount Hermon. Nearer, on a jutting rock to the left, they saw the white marble temple which Herod the Great had built to exalt the divinity of Caesar Augustus, though the region lay within ancient Israel.

In this setting where pagan myth, Roman power, and the lost glories of Israel were alike dwarfed by Hermon, Jesus taught the Twelve privately. As John listened while the hours sped by, he had a sense that Jesus wanted to draw them out and to make them face the deeper implications of discipleship; but before John could formulate his thoughts, Jesus turned to prayer. To be present when he prayed, in the intimate, unaffected way they knew so well, John felt was the greatest privilege of all, and when the prayer ended, a great peace held heart and mind. But Jesus did not resume his teaching. Instead, he asked a question, "Who do men say that I am?"

John was sure that Jesus knew the excited, puzzled, admiring guesses of the lakeside crowds, but several disciples repeated them. "Some say, 'John the Baptist!' "—the rumor that Herod Antipas, disturbed by his guilty conscience when he heard about miracles, had declared, that the Baptist must have come back from the dead.

"Others say you are Elijah!"

"Or the Prophet Jeremiah!" The popular explanation always involved the return to earth of a dead hero.

"What about you?" asked Jesus. "Who do *you* say that I am?"

In the fishing boat after he had walked on water, they had blurted out that he was Son of God. At Capernaum when many abandoned him, Peter had called him the "Holy One of God," but these were emotional responses to moments of crisis. Jesus now wanted a clear affirmation from which there could be no going back; and since lies and half-truths were impossible to utter in his presence, they must say what they believed, however absurd it might sound in the ordinary world of men and boats and fish markets.

John was still trying to frame words to express his personal certainty when suddenly Peter bounded toward Jesus. Looking as if an instant vision had blazed the truth into his mind, he cried: "You are the Christ! The Son of the Living God!"

Jesus looked at Peter with the utmost earnestness and authority. "Simon, son of Jonah," he said, "you are blessed indeed. For this was not revealed to you by man but by my Father in heaven. And you are Peter, the rock, and on this rock I will build my church, which hell itself shall never defeat."

Across the valley, the other rock, with its fine temple to Caesar, seemed to mock such a prophecy, but Jesus went on to promise, very solemnly, to give Peter the keys of the kingdom of heaven. All the Twelve knew that in a royal palace the king's most responsible servant carried the keys as a mark of his authority. Peter, carrying out God's directions, would declare the Gospel which loosed the sins of some while others remained bound. Then Jesus turned to the others and, to their astonishment, warned them all not to trumpet abroad who he was.

He led them away from the Springs of Pan and the Rock of Augustus. They spent the days after Peter's confession walking together in the foothills of Mount Hermon and near the villages of Caesarea Philippi. Jesus impressed upon them that the immediate future bore no relation to any dream they might have that he, as the Messiah whom every Jew awaited, would come swiftly to glory and power with his chosen companions in splendor at his side. He told them that they would be going to Jerusalem; that he would be abused, insulted, and maltreated by the elders and chief priests and the teachers of the Law; that he must be killed, "and on the third day be raised to life."

They did not take him seriously. Jesus repeated the teaching until at length they were left in no doubt that he did not speak in a parable but of what would happen.

Peter was horrified. The Christ, even if they must not reveal Jesus as such, would have unlimited power to prevent His own death. Besides, Jesus' moral goodness and beauty of character could not deserve death. Peter drew Jesus aside. They were near a village, and the crowds had increased, since his fame always caught up with him; and Peter did not want inquisitive ears to catch any hint that Jesus expected to be insulted and killed.

Once out of earshot, Peter spoke his mind. "Never," he said. "Never, Lord! These things shall never happen to you!"

Jesus walked on as if not hearing. Peter ran after him. "Never, never, never," he began again. Jesus turned, and Peter's words froze at the look on Jesus' face.

With such force that Peter trembled, Jesus rebuked him. "Out of my sight, Satan! You are a stumbling block to me. There is a smell of man about you, not the scent of God."

Jesus called the other disciples to gather round and beckoned all the people to hear, thus defeating Peter's intention of secrecy.

"If any of you want to follow me, you must say no to yourself and take up your cross and follow me!" John's heart chilled as he recalled the too familiar sight of a criminal, convicted by Roman law, struggling under a crossbeam toward a place of execution. John had seen a man stripped and iron nails hammered through his wrists or hands to the beam he had carried; screaming, he was lifted roughly on to the upright timber already in place and died slowly in fearful pain.

Jesus was speaking with unmistakable emphasis. "Whoever wants to save his life will lose it," he said. "Whoever loses his life *for me* will find it." It was no good if a man gained all that this world could offer, yet lost his own soul. "If anyone is ashamed of me and of my words in this adulterous and sinful generation, the Son of man will be ashamed of him when he comes in his Father's glory with the holy angels."

He dismissed the crowd and again led the Twelve into the foothills, where they camped the short summer nights under the cedars and spent daytime in seclusion while he taught them.

During the afternoon of the sixth day, while they all rested in the shade, John heard Jesus calling him by name. He called James and Peter too. Telling the others to await their return, he led the three along a rough track through vineyards to the higher pastures and up the ridge which climbs steadily northwest toward the summits of Hermon. They emerged from clumps of cedars to the region of scrub, then threaded their way easily through ravines on hard-packed snow.

They stopped to rest. The silence and the wildness and the isolation—since the coastal plain and the Jordan Valley were hidden by heat haze—made a perfect setting for Jesus to let his three closest friends into secret memories which they would not have understood before Peter's confession. He told them of the voice from heaven which he had heard as he came up from the Jordan water at his baptism: "You are my beloved Son. I am well pleased with you." This strengthened their conviction of who he was.

They continued their climb. The sun on the rocks and snow patches made the afternoon even hotter, and they stopped again by a stream which hurried down from the heights. Here, Jesus told of the arid wilderness of Judea where he had gone after his baptism, to be locked for forty days in a mental and spiritual battle. He spoke of temptation which John could barely comprehend, as all the evil that assaulted or deceived mankind converged: cruelty, lust, despair—whatever was contrary to the character of Jesus yet common to man.

It had mounted to a climax with three successive assaults. Toward the end of his long fast, Jesus said, he had become hungry. Some of the stones in that part of the mountains looked like loaves: they needed only the touch of God. The tempter said, "If you are the Son of God, tell these stones to become bread," and what he did in solitude for his own relief Jesus could do for others, swiftly meeting the physical needs of mankind and buying their adoration.

That was not his way. Jesus told of destroying the temptation by a quotation from Scripture: "Man does not live by bread alone, but on every word that comes from the mouth of God."

Next the devil had taken him to a high mountain. As Jesus told this on Hermon, the haze was lifting, and John could see the glint of the Sea of Galilee forty miles to the south and the Mediterranean to the west. Jesus had often spoken in parables, and nothing seemed strange to his three friends when he recounted how the devil had shown him in a flash all the kingdoms of the world and their glory, and had promised: "I will give you all their authority and splendor, for it has been given to me, and I can give it to anyone I want to. So if you will fall down and worship me, all shall be yours."

Again Jesus had refuted him from Scripture: "It is written, 'Worship the Lord your God and serve him only.'" Jesus refused to win the world as the devil's viceroy, making evil triumph forever.

John listened, enraptured. He had noticed the compassion of Jesus for men and women who suffered assaults of evil, but he never had conceived what Jesus had been through himself.

The third struggle had taken place on the pinnacle of the Temple, at the southeast corner above the royal colonnade, the pinnacle from which a blasphemer sentenced to death was thrown into the ravine. "If," said the devil to Jesus, "you *are* the Son of God, throw yourself down. It is written: 'He will command his angels to guard you carefully. They will lift you up in their hands so that you do not crash upon the stones.' " Jesus, the devil implied, would demonstrate that he was not a blasphemer and the people would flock to him. Above all, this would test his Father's love and care.

Jesus killed the temptation by yet another quotation, again from the Book of Deuteronomy: "Do not put the Lord your God to the test." Jesus had no need to test his Father's love: he was conscious of him always and clung to him.

Satan fled the field—for a time, said Jesus. Satan would return when the time was ripe, a prospect which dismayed the disciples listening on Hermon. But they believed their Master to be more powerful than all the powers of hell and took comfort too from his disclosure that he knew what it was to be tempted.

Evening was nearly on them. Jesus led them higher, almost to one of the summits, more than 11,000 feet above the Jordan. They sat on a broad ledge a little below an ancient ruined temple of Baal, where they were out of the breeze. The sun sinking into the Mediterranean bathed them in its glow; then darkness fell suddenly and the stars and a quarter moon appeared; in stillness and peace, heaven and earth seemed at one.

Jesus withdrew a few paces, lifted his face, and began to pray, sometimes silently, sometimes aloud. An hour passed as if in moments, and John wrapped himself closer in his cloak, determined to stay with Jesus in mind and heart all night if he wished, and James and Peter felt the same. But the climb up Hermon had been long. They were tired and had not eaten, and despite themselves they dozed, then fell asleep.

John was awakened by light. When he looked up, it was not yet dawn; the light came from Jesus as he prayed. John shaded his eyes, almost in terror, for Jesus' face shone like the sun, and his clothes were brilliant, dazzling white, like lightning. None of the three could find adequate words to describe the experience afterward: "We saw his glory."/"We were eyewitnesses of his majesty."

To their astonishment, Jesus was not alone. High on that mountain as the disciples became fully awake, they saw two resplendent figures speaking with Jesus. John listened as they talked; and he knew, without doubt, that the barrier between time and eternity had torn away, and that one was Moses, the long-dead lawgiver, and the other, Elijah, the long-dead prophet: John knew by the words they spoke, for he had never seen their portraits or sculpture, since images were forbidden to Jews.

The two patriarchs plainly regarded Jesus as their superior, yet he seemed to be drawing strength from them. They were talking about the way Jesus would depart from the earth. John, James, and Peter heard and understood the words but could no more accept the theme than they had accepted it from Jesus himself: that while yet young, Jesus would be disgraced and killed at Jerusalem like a common criminal, whereas Moses and Elijah had each gone to heaven gloriously, after a long life's work.

Suddenly Peter interrupted, blurting, "Lord! Let us make three shelters—one for you, one for Moses, one for Elijah!" He said it without thought. He was neither trying to preserve the moment nor reducing Jesus to the level of the patriarchs; it was Peter at his most impulsive.

Even as he spoke, they saw a cloud coming up fast, not the mountain mist before dawn but a cloud so intensely bright that the three disciples fell on their faces in terror. Instinctively, they recognized the cloud of glory which, at special times of divine revelation in the history of the people of Israel had veiled God's holiness from sinful man.

A voice irresistibly penetrated their consciousness: "This is

My beloved Son, whom I have chosen; hear him."

John did not dare look up. He lay drained of strength and pride. . . .

John felt a touch on the shoulder. In familiar, comforting tones Jesus said: "Get up. Don't be afraid."

Dawn had broken. Jesus was alone. He now looked as they had always known him.

Thirteen
ON THE ROAD

Coming down the mountain, the three disciples—John, James, and Peter—did not share their thoughts, but John believed what Peter expressed, long afterward, that in their presence Jesus had received honor from God the Father by the voice and the glory. They had a story to tell that they believed would make every man worship their friend.

When they paused for a brief rest, Jesus ordered them not to give the slightest hint of what they had seen and heard, "until the Son of man has risen from the dead." They puzzled over his meaning yet obeyed his instructions, and during the next months suppressed the memory so effectively that sometimes they behaved as if they had never been present at his Transfiguration.

They continued their descent and emerged from the cedar forest. Below them, at the place where they had left the nine others, they noticed a crowd. When they were nearly down and plainly visible, a man of about thirty-five broke away and ran uphill toward Jesus and threw himself on his knees, his face a picture of agitation.

The man cried: "Teacher, I brought you my son. He suddenly screams and goes into a fit. He is deprived of speech and hearing. He is my only child, and the demon that has got into him is destroying him. I brought him to your disciples and they could not heal him."

Jesus sighed. "What an unbelieving and perverse generation!" he exclaimed. "How long shall I stay among you and put up with you? Bring the boy to me."

The boy walked normally until he reached Jesus, then fell to the ground and rolled about, foaming at the mouth.

Jesus asked how long he had been afflicted. "From childhood," the father replied. Then he described how the boy had frequently nearly burned to death or drowned. "But if you can, take pity on us and help us!" he added.

" 'If you can?' " echoed Jesus. "Everything is possible to those who believe!"

The father cried, "I believe! Help my unbelief."

The onlookers were now running to the place where the boy lay having a fit.

Jesus spoke sternly to the unclean spirit in the boy: "Get out, I command you, and never enter him again."

The boy shrieked and went into a convulsion, then lay inert. The onlookers began to murmur that he was dead. After a few moments Jesus bent down and lifted him tenderly to his feet. The boy opened his eyes, looked around, and smiled. Jesus handed him back, healed and normal, to the father. The people were astonished.

Jesus immediately led the Twelve away. "Why couldn't we do it?" complained the nine. Jesus replied that such a case could be healed only by fasting and prayer. He did not pursue the subject but began to emphasize once again that he was going to be betrayed into the hands of men, to be killed, "and rise again after three days." As they walked back to Galilee by the quiet bypaths which he chose, he taught them on this theme, but they could not grasp his meaning and were afraid to ask questions.

They seemed almost out of sympathy. Jesus was quiet and serious as if walking toward suffering, but the Twelve were bursting with self-importance derived from certainty now that he was the Son of God and they his chosen helpers. John and Peter kept their promise not to tell of their recent experience, but could not disguise their conviction that they would be vice-regents when he ascended the throne. An argument even developed as to who would be the greatest; fortunately, Jesus was walking a little way ahead and appeared not to notice.

They reached Capernaum and entered Peter's house to be welcomed by wives and families. Suddenly Jesus asked, "What were you arguing about on the road?" The disciples looked sheepish. Jesus sat down and made the Twelve gather round. "If anyone wants to be first," he said, "he must be the very last, and the servant of all."

Then he called one of the small children—perhaps Peter's youngest—and had him stand at his knees. Jesus put his arms round him and gently drove the lesson home.

"Whoever," he said, "welcomes this little child in my name welcomes me, and whoever welcomes me welcomes the one who sent me. For he who is least among you all—he is the greatest."

John tried to cover their shame by stressing their zeal. "Master," he said proudly, "we saw a man driving out demons in your name, and we stopped him, because he was not one of us."

John had merely floundered deeper. Jesus rebuked him again: "Do not stop him, for whoever is not against us is for us."

Soon afterward Jesus set out for Jerusalem with a determination which impressed all his friends that he was going toward the climax of his life. He turned away from the Sea of Galilee as if he would never see it again, and led the Twelve, with the large company of men and women who wished to accompany him, into the Galilean hills toward the direct route through Samaria. Theirs was a big caravan, all on foot. Each evening, before they reached a village where they might camp or stay in homes, Jesus sent messengers ahead to arrange hospitality. At one village on the border, they came back rebuffed: it was peopled by Samaritans who refused pilgrims bound for Jerusalem.

John and James were standing with Jesus when the messengers reported. John was furious that his Master should be insulted. He and James, still puffed by their experience on Mount Hermon, wanted to vindicate him. "Shall we call down fire from heaven to destroy them?" he demanded, silently recalling how Elijah had saved himself when an evil king dispatched soldiers to arrest him.

Jesus turned and rebuked the brothers. His look pricked their pride and disarmed their violence yet assured them that he understood their love. He led them all to another village.

He seemed in no hurry to reach Jerusalem. The journey became a medley of memories as John looked back: He remembered the day, for instance, when they were nearing a village on the Samaritan border, and John heard men calling out, from a distance, in unison, "Jesus, Master! Have mercy on us."

Jesus had stopped. John had seen a group of ten unkempt outcasts, whose rags and long hair, and reluctance to come nearer, betrayed them as lepers.

Jesus called back, his voice strong and clear: "Go and show yourselves to the priests!" They ran off toward their own village while Jesus walked on. Some time later John heard the sound of a man shouting praises to God in an excited voice, and one of these long-haired outcasts pushed his way through the crowd, flung himself at Jesus' feet, and poured out his thanks. The ten men had been on their way to the priests, he said, when they became aware that they were healed. He himself had at once turned back.

Jesus noticed that this man was a Samaritan, and looking around he said: "Where are the other men whom I healed? Has none of them returned to give God praise except this foreigner? Then he looked down at the grateful man kneeling at his feet. "Stand up and go; your faith has made you well."

In contrast, on another day a glib fellow ambled up to Jesus as he and his disciples walked along. The man announced dramatically, "I will follow you wherever you go!" Jesus was not impressed. "Foxes have holes and birds have nests," he replied, "but the Son of man has nowhere to lay his head." Nothing more was heard of the man.

Yet another day Jesus had risen early and gone a little way into the fields. John and the closest disciples had followed, partly to protect him but mainly to share the beauty and peace which they knew would linger as he prayed. The simple intimacy of his prayers highlighted their feeble struggles to reach God; when Jesus ended, one of them recalled how John the Baptist had given lessons in prayer to his disciples, and the disciple said to Jesus, "Lord, teach us to pray."

Jesus took the several disciples back to the whole company, then met the request. He told them to pray in these words:

Our Father in heaven, hallowed be your name. Your kingdom come; your will be done, on earth as it is in heaven. Give us this day our daily bread. Forgive us our trespasses, as we forgive them that trespass against us. Lead us not into temptation but deliver us from evil.

Then the disciples repeated the teaching phrase by phrase after Jesus as they sat round him on the roadside. Posterity would call this—in reality the disciples' prayer—the Lord's Prayer—the single most quoted passage of all Jesus' sayings—words which, as the Christian faith spread across the world, would be prayed every day, year after year through all the centuries to come.

Jesus taught his disciples the phrases, but he stressed that God really wanted to know their detailed needs. With vivid stories he urged them to come boldly to their Heavenly Father. "Ask and it will be given you; seek and you will find; knock and the door will be opened to you. You fathers, if your son asks for bread, will you give him a stone? Or for a fish, will you give him a snake? . . . If you, who are evil, know how to give good gifts to your children, how much more will your Father in heaven give the Holy Spirit to those who ask him!"

One day he found in his audience many tax collectors who had grown rich, like Matthew before his call, by legalized extortion on behalf of the occupying power. Jesus showed at once that he did not ignore them because they were neither poor nor helpless; he welcomed them and accepted their hospitality. At this, the local Pharisees and doctors of the Law began to mutter. Jesus therefore addressed these first, putting the issue in the form of a parable.

"Suppose one of you," he said, "owns a hundred sheep and one gets lost. Does he not leave the ninety-nine in the open pasture and go after the one lost sheep until he finds it? And then he lays it on his shoulder and comes home rejoicing. He calls his friends and neighbors together: 'Rejoice with me. I have found the sheep which was lost.' "

He added a similar parable of a woman who lost a silver coin and swept until she found it and then called in the neighbors to celebrate.

After each story, Jesus drove home the point: "I tell you, there is more joy in heaven over one sinner who repents than over ninety-nine righteous persons who do not need to repent."

Then Jesus turned back to the taxgatherers and began the immortal story of the Prodigal Son, the young man who asked his father for his share of the inheritance and went to a far country and wasted his substance with riotous living. After he had spent all, a famine came and he was reduced to feeding pigs. Jesus continued:

"And when the younger son came to himself he said, 'How many hired servants of my father's have bread enough and to spare, and I perish with hunger! I will arise and go to my father, and will say to him, "Father, I have sinned against heaven and before you, and am no more worthy to be called your son; make me as one of your hired servants." '

"And he arose and came to his father. But when he was yet a great way off, his father saw him, and had compassion on him, and ran, and fell on his neck, and kissed him.

"And the son said unto him, 'Father, I have sinned against heaven and in your sight, and am no more worthy to be called your son.'

"But the father commanded his servants, 'Bring forth the best robe and put it on him; and put a ring on his hand and shoes on his feet; and bring hither the fatted calf and kill it; and let us eat and celebrate with a feast! For this my son was dead and is alive again; he was lost and is found!' And they began to prepare for the celebration."

Jesus rounded off the story telling of the surly elder brother, cross because the prodigal had been so warmly received, refusing to join the music and dancing to celebrate. The elder brother's character fitted the Pharisees and doctors of the Law who were listening, amazed that Jesus should speak of compassion rather than of wrath, of repentance, restoration, and joy.

This and other stories made the hours fly by and drew such crowds that people trod upon one another. Jesus balanced the parables by straight teaching, addressed primarily to his disciples. He condemned hypocrisy and did not hesitate to rebuke powerful religious leaders; he warned of coming judgment; he provided clear lessons for life in its every aspect in a harsh world; and he pictured a future when sin and crime and greed would have disappeared from the earth.

To John, this seemed only a dream, leaving intolerable longing, but the words were spoken by Jesus, whom he knew to be no empty dreamer but a man of action and purpose. John could not conceive of how all of this would come about, and neither did he understand Jesus' talk of being killed and coming alive again after three days. Once, in deep emotion, Jesus burst out with strange words: "I have come to bring fire on the earth, and how I wish it were already kindled! But I have a baptism to undergo, and how distressed I am until it is completed! Do you think I came to bring peace on earth? No, I tell you, but rather I came to bring division."

Neither John, nor other disciples, nor the people knew what Jesus meant. They sensed only that his face was set toward Jerusalem.

At last the band of travelers approached the final ascent

from Jericho, a wild road, infested with brigands. Jesus made it the setting for his parable of the Good Samaritan later when a crowd gathered about him.

He told it because a lawyer put a test question to him: "What must I do to inherit eternal life?"

Jesus turned the question. He asked the lawyer what he read in the Law of Moses. The people listened intently as the lawyer recited part of the great declaration heard during every synagogue service: "Love the Lord your God with all your heart, and with all your soul, and with all your strength, and with all your mind." To regain the initiative, the lawyer added, from a different book of Moses, "*And* your neighbor as yourself."

Jesus replied, "You have answered correctly. Do this and you will live." The people tittered, for the lawyer had opened himself to receive a glimpse of the obvious.

He would not concede defeat. "And who is my neighbor?" he asked sneering.

Instead of embarking on a debate of the kind relished by lawyers and scribes, Jesus began a story. He told of a man who went down from Jerusalem to Jericho and fell into the hands of robbers. They stripped him, beat him, and went away leaving him half dead by the roadside. Several travelers came on the scene: First, a priest, hurried by on the other side (lest he be defiled by touching what might be a corpse). Then came a Levite, one of the Temple singers and servants; he also thought it wiser to pass by on the other side.

The third traveler, Jesus said, was a Samaritan. The audience despised Samaritans and would expect no good of him. But, Jesus continued, the Samaritan "came where the man was; and when he saw him, he took pity on him. He went to him and bandaged his wounds, pouring on oil and wine." He put him on his own donkey and carried him to the nearest inn and took care of him, and on leaving next day the Samaritan paid the innkeeper to keep the victim until he had recovered.

"Which of these three," asked Jesus, reversing the lawyer's question, "do you think was a neighbor to the man who fell among thieves?"

"The one who had mercy on him," admitted the lawyer.

"Then go and do likewise," said Jesus.

The lawyer said no more.

Fourteen
A MAN
BORN BLIND

At the head of the road, hidden from Jerusalem by the flank of the Mount of Olives, lay the village of Bethany. When Jesus and his disciples stopped to rest after their climb, the Master was invited by one of the principal residents, a woman named Martha, to be her guest. He no longer had a large crowd at his heels because many of the Galileans had hurried ahead to the city for the start of the Feast of Tabernacles, the national thanksgiving for the harvests, held annually before the autumn rains.

Led by Martha and her sister, Mary, Jesus walked to their substantial home, with the Twelve following a little behind. Like all Jewish householders in the Jerusalem district who had the space, Martha and Mary had set up a tabernacle or booth of palm fronds adjacent to their home for the week of the festival, according to ancient custom. The booth opened to the garden. Martha showed Jesus to a couch in the booth and hurried off to supervise the preparation of the meal. Mary was about to follow when she noticed the Twelve gather round as if expecting Jesus to continue his teaching. She waited, and he began. Mary came close and the others made way for her, and she sat on the ground at his feet listening intently. She lost all sense of time. Suddenly Martha bustled out of the house and into the booth, interrupting Jesus. "Lord, don't you care that my sister has left me to do the work by myself? Tell her to help me!"

Jesus looked up at Martha, her brow knotted and her face flushed from her efforts, her sleeves were rolled up to the elbows. Then he looked down at Mary, absorbed and at peace. He turned back to Martha. His smile and the way he spoke took the sting out of his rebuke: "Martha, Martha, you are fretting and fussing about so many things, but one thing is needed. Mary has chosen the best part, and it shall not be taken away from her."

Martha smiled at Jesus, smiled at Mary, and went back inside the house without bustle. Evidently, she finished preparations less elaborately, for she soon brought out the meal to the booth, all grumbles forgotten. The sisters both served happily. Their brother, Lazarus, had arrived from Jerusalem, and from his first meeting with Jesus a warm friendship began.

Jesus did not remain overnight. He preferred to conform to the custom of pilgrims to the festival, from all over Palestine and countries far and near, and stay in one of the numerous temporary booths of palm fronds on the Mount of Olives. Next day he did not go into the city. As he had said in Galilee when his unbelieving half brothers taunted him to attend the feast in a flourish of self-advertisement, his time had not yet come.

John went to find out what people were saying. As he passed through the great walls and up into the magnificence of the Temple courts, he saw the smoke of sacrifices ascending from the altar. At festival time, and all through the year on a lesser scale, the priests killed bullocks, goats, or lambs offered by worshipers. Man's sins could be purged only by the shedding of blood; therefore, the innocent must die that the sinner might live.

By conversation with priests and nobles known to his family, John learned that the unofficial decision to destroy Jesus, taken after he had healed the paralyzed man at the Pool of Bethesda, had not been rescinded; the rulers were watching out for him, since all males were supposed to appear at this festival. Among the crowds John heard plenty of gossip. Some said Jesus was a good man, others that he led the people astray, but no one dared refer to him publicly lest they be accused of being his disciples.

John reported his findings to Jesus, who still did not leave the Mount of Olives. On the fourth day of the festival week, he came into the city quietly and went to the Temple and sat down to teach under one of the porticoes of the great Court of the Gentiles. The court was noisy with merchants buying and selling and the bleating of sheep to be bought for sacrifice, but it was the traditional place for teachers who sought an audience.

Jesus soon had people gathered about him. Those who never had heard him were amazed. It was plain to most that he had not sat under any famous rabbi, for each school had its mannerisms, yet he displayed a learning which outclassed them by its simplicity, depth, and authority. Some among the crowd who knew that the Pharisees wanted to kill him were astonished that Jesus could speak freely. "Have they concluded that he is the Messiah?" they asked. Others scoffed at the idea because they knew that he came from Galilee, whereas, they said, the origin of the Messiah, or Christ, would be a mystery.

As he taught, Jesus made claims which aroused wrath. For instance, he said: "I am not here of my own accord, but he who sent me is true. You do not know him, but I know him because I come from him and he sent me." John saw several Pharisees lurch forward as if to seize him, only to stop as if some invisible power prevented them.

On the last day of the festival, the ceremonies climaxed with joyful processions of worshipers waving branches. Trumpets sounded. Priests poured out wine and water from golden ewers to symbolize prayer for rain. The people sang pslams of praise.

As the singing died away, Jesus cried out in a voice which carried right across the crowd and up to the curtained Holy of Holies: "If any man is thirsty, let him come to me and drink. Anyone who believes in me, rivers of living water shall flow from within him as the Scripture says."

John did not fully understand at that moment, nor for another seven months, but he realized that Jesus had stated unashamedly that he was the source of true spiritual life. His face and tones showed that he longed to draw all Jerusalem, and indeed the world, to himself.

Reaction was mixed, but Temple guards who were sent to arrest him stood open-mouthed in admiration, until John saw them clank away. He heard afterward that they had excused their disobedience by saying, "No one ever spoke like this man."

In the days after the Feast of Tabernacles, Jesus did not depart for the countryside with most of the pilgrims. His friendship with Lazarus, Martha, and Mary gave him a base of warm hospitality from which to face hostility.

The conflict between Jesus and the authorities grew more intense as he made claims which they could not ignore. They must accept them and acknowledge him, or suppress him by argument or force. No other prophet had made such claims for himself. One confrontation especially impressed itself on John. Jesus had gone again to the Temple. He led them to the Court of the Women, and took his seat under a portico near the trumpet-shaped offering chests, where a steady stream of worshipers came to drop in their Temple contributions and stay to listen to him. Pharisees were already there, shadowing him.

"I am the Light of the world," he taught. "Anybody who follows me will never walk in darkness but will have the light of life."

The Pharisees started to argue, but the more they tried to refute or insult him the more firmly he held his ground. He assured his hearers that when they had killed him, "you will know that I am what I am. I do nothing on my own authority; I speak what the Father taught me. He who sent me is present with me. He has not left me alone, *because I always do what pleases him.*"

Jesus said it with such simplicity and authority, not as a boast but as a fact, that many believed in him. However, they would not go the whole way; when he told them that if they followed his teaching, "you will know the truth, and the truth will set you free," they retorted that as Abraham's descendants they had never been slaves. The religious leaders started to argue again. Jesus did not retreat. They were children of the father of lies, he said, and therefore did not believe when Jesus told the truth. He made an even stronger statement: "Which of you can prove me guilty of sin?"

They hurled insults at him: he was a Samaritan and demon possessed.

"I am not demon possessed," replied Jesus calmly. A little later he made the solemn declaration: "If a man keeps my word, he will never see death."

The leaders erupted with scorn. "Now we know you are demon possessed! Abraham died, the prophets died, and yet you say this! Are you greater than our father Abraham? Who do you think you are?"

Jesus parried the question. If he exalted himself it meant nothing; he replied, "My Father, whom you claim as your God, is the one who glorifies me. You do not know him. I do. If I denied it I would be a liar—like you. But I know him. I keep his word. Your father Abraham rejoiced to see my day. He saw it and was glad."

"What!" they said. "You are not yet fifty years old and *you have seen Abraham?*"

"In very truth," replied Jesus, "before Abraham was born, *I am*"—the sacred phrase which, in the Scriptures, God alone used. He had claimed to be God! They could bear no more. They rushed toward a pile of building stones to stone the blasphemer to death without trial.

Jesus slipped away out of the Temple.

A day or two later, a Sabbath, he was in the city with John, Peter, and a few of the others when they saw a blind beggar sitting by the streetside, well placed for the charitable on their way to the Temple. He was a man of about thirty, in rags, who called out, "Born blind, born blind."

One of the disciples voiced the traditional view of affliction as punishment, and with no regard for the man's self-respect, asked Jesus unfeelingly whom he thought had sinned, the man or his parents. Jesus replied that neither had sinned; the beggar was born blind so that a work of God could be displayed. The man lifted his head inquiringly as he heard Jesus say: "We must do God's work while it is day.

Night is coming, when no one can work. While I am in the world, I am the Light of the world."

Jesus spat on the dusty ground, kneaded some mud with his saliva, and plastered the man's eyes. Two of these actions broke Sabbath prohibitions. He ordered, "Go and wash in the Pool of Siloam." Without hesitation the man seized his stick, left his begging bowl, and tapped away down the street for the long walk to the pool at the lower end of the city.

Next day the story was all over Jerusalem. The beggar had gone home that Sabbath from the Pool of Siloam, his sight restored, and his neighbors were astounded that he could see as well as they. They were even more astonished when they heard his story. They had him interrogated by Pharisees.

These met their match. The once-blind man surmised that they were less interested in the miracle than in obtaining the evidence against Jesus for breaking the Sabbath, and he was spirited, even saucy in his replies. After examining his parents, who were afraid to say much, they adjured the beggar to tell the truth, for "we know this man is a sinner."

The beggar refused to be browbeaten. "Whether he is a sinner or not, I don't know. What I do know is: I was once blind but now I see!"

They started to question him again on the facts of his cure. He retorted, "I have told you once and you did not listen. Why do you want to hear it again? Do you want to become his disciples too?"

The Pharisees reviled him. He then had the audacity to lecture them, concluding, "If this man were not from God, he could do nothing."

The Pharisees suddenly became furious. "You were altogether born in sin," they said, and threw him out, so that he would not be allowed to attend synagogue. He risked formal excommunication, with all the social and material loss which would follow.

Jesus heard what had happened. He took John and others to find him; beggars who had been with the man could tell them where to look. When they met, Jesus asked him, "Do you believe in the Son of man?"

The beggar had never set eyes on Jesus, but with instinctive respect he replied, "Who is he, Sir, that I might believe?"

"You have seen him. He is talking with you now!"

"Lord," replied the man, falling at Jesus' feet, "I believe!"

The cure of the man born blind impressed Jerusalem deeply, but the miracle strengthened the resolve of the Jewish authorities to rid themselves of Jesus.

He spoke openly of his death: "I am the Good Shepherd," he said, in the course of a sermon which would remain among his greatest. "The Good Shepherd gives his life for the sheep." Later in the sermon he uttered an even stronger reference, though neither John nor any of the Twelve could fully understand or accept it. He had told his audience that he had sheep of other folds to bring into his flock. "They too must hear my voice, and there will be one flock and one shepherd. My Father loves me," he went on, "because I lay down my life, to take it up again. No one takes my life from me. I lay it down of my own accord. I have power to lay it down and power to take it again. I have received this command from my Father."

Some of his hearers reckoned him mad and not worth hearing. Others remembered the man born blind.

At last, in midwinter, when all Jerusalem was bright with lights to celebrate the recovery of the Temple from pagan defilement long ago, the Jewish elders demanded, "Tell us plainly. Are you the Christ?"

"I did tell you, but you do not believe," because they were not his sheep. "My sheep hear my voice and I give them eternal life. They shall never perish. No one can pluck them out of my hand." His questioners listened with mounting disbelief and fury, all the fiercer because Jesus spoke without rhetoric, as a man of integrity who cannot swerve from truth.

When he said, "I and my Father are one," they contained their anger no longer. They picked up stones to fling at him.

He stood still. "For which miracle are you stoning me?"

"Not for a miracle," they cried, "but for blasphemy! Because you, a man, make yourself out to be God!"

Fifteen
LAZARUS

With great sadness Jesus left the city and took his disciples down the steep road to Jericho and across the Jordan into Perea, which like Galilee was ruled by Herod.

Many came out from Jericho and the villages on the Jordan. They remembered vividly the Baptist's preaching in that very place and agreed that all he had said about Jesus was true. Others came down from Jerusalem. As the days passed, John saw more and more listeners believe in Jesus and range themselves at his side. John also kept open his contacts with Jerusalem, and men in high quarters warned that the chief priests remained implacably his foes, inflamed by reports coming up from Jordan. Jesus must avoid Judea.

Toward the end of winter a man pushed through the crowd after hurrying down the mountain road. He carried an urgent message from Martha and Mary about Lazarus. "Lord, your great friend is sick." Jesus at once shared this cry for help, already many hours old because of its journey. John was by now used to the impression that Jesus always knew more than anyone told him, but when he said, "This sickness will not end in death. It is going to glorify God by glorifying his son," none of the disciples could fathom Jesus' meaning. He made no move. Since Jesus loved Mary, Martha, and Lazarus, John wondered whether Lazarus had recovered. Other disciples suggested that Jesus had healed from a distance, without touch, as he had done before.

Jesus spent much time by himself in prayer. Two days passed. Then he announced that they would go back to Judea.

"The Jews tried to stone you!" the Twelve objected. "Must you go back already?"

Jesus replied in picture language that they could walk safely because it was still daylight; night was coming but not yet. He said, "Our friend Lazarus has fallen asleep. I go to wake him."

When they supposed he meant natural sleep, Jesus dropped his picture language. "Lazarus is dead! And I am glad I was not there, for your sakes, because this is going to strengthen your faith. Come on, we must start."

"Let's go too," said Thomas gloomily, "so that we may die with him."

A day afterward, having climbed the road without haste, Jesus and his nervous disciples reached the edge of Bethany. They discovered at once that Lazarus had died four days earlier, before the messenger could reach them, and had been laid in his tomb by sunset.

Jesus sat down on a low wall. He would not enter Bethany; instead, he sent a message to the sisters by John, who heard the customary wailing as he reached their house. The three days of violent grief which began a month of mourn-

ing were over, but he saw furniture up-ended, hired mourners on the floor making loud lamentations, and neighbors
and friends still coming in to offer condolences and then to
join the wailing. Many prominent Jews had made the short
journey from Jerusalem.

Martha was preparing food. She left at once, without telling Mary, who was inside among the mourners, and John
ran with her. On reaching Jesus, she did not waste a moment
in greeting, or in thanks for his coming, but unburdened her
misery. "Lord, if only you had been here, my brother would
not have died." The thought had haunted her and Mary the
past four days. "But," she went on, "I know that even now,
God will give you whatever you ask."

Jesus said to her, "Your brother will rise again."

She misunderstood. "Yes, in the resurrection at the last
day. I know that."

He looked at her intently. He took her wrist, as if to
prepare her for something that would test her faith to the
uttermost. "Martha," he said, "*I* am the Resurrection, and
the life. Anyone who believes in me will live even though he
dies."

John could see this tremendous claim sink into Martha's
mind: words which would be quoted all over the world in
centuries to come, wherever a Christian's corpse awaited
burial, heard first on the edge of Bethany under the Mount
of Olives on a late winter's day. "The Resurrection is—*me*.
Life is—*me*."

Jesus held Martha's gaze as he continued. "Anyone who
lives believing in me will never die. Do you believe this?"

"Yes, Lord. I believe." And John heard her say softly what
Peter had blurted out: "You are the Christ, the Son of God,
who was promised to come into the world."

"Fetch Mary," said Jesus.

Without another word, dropping all protest at his delay, all her implied demand for action, she obeyed. John could not grasp any more than Martha what Jesus intended, but a little later he saw Mary hurrying toward them, her face wet with tears. Martha was beside her, and behind came a gaggle of mourners who had supposed that Mary intended to wail at the tomb.

Mary fell at Jesus' feet. "If only," she said through her tears, "you had been here, Lord, my brother would not have died."

The tears fell hot on his feet. The mourners held back, wailing with simulated grief or weeping silently, heartbroken with the sisters.

John looked at Jesus and saw that he was moved to the depths. His body shook. A great groan came from far within, of sympathy beyond words and hatred of death and all that caused death.

"Where have you laid him?" Jesus asked.

"Come and see, Lord," replied the sisters, and led him toward the garden on the side of the hill. As they walked, Jesus wept. The sisters clung to him, drawing strength from his tears.

The mourners and the disciples followed. John heard a mourner murmur, "See how much he loved him." Others recalled the blind man in Jerusalem and wondered why Jesus could not have saved Lazarus.

They reached the garden. A great stone lay across the entrance to a cave set in the hillside. Again, Jesus groaned, his whole body moving, as if tensing for great spiritual and physical exertion.

"Take away the stone!"

"But he stinks, Lord!" cried Martha. "He has been there four days!" If Jesus wanted to enter for a last look, the stench of decay would be stronger now than the spices, for they did not embalm like the ancient Egyptians. She could think of no other reason for the command. Lazarus was beyond help; the Jews believed that the spirit hovered near the body for three days and then departed. Lazarus was dead indeed.

Jesus said, "Did I not tell you that if you believed, you would see the glory of God?"

Younger mourners heaved at the stone and shifted it. Jesus wanted it moved away, as if to emphasize that it would not be needed again. The cave ran into the rock face deep and high; at the burial the bearers had not needed to stoop.

Jesus lifted his eyes upward. "Father," he said. A stillness fell upon the little crowd; wails and weeping stopped. "Father, thank you. Thank you that you have heard me. I know you always hear me, but I am giving my thanks to help the people standing here, that from now on they may believe that you sent me."

Then with a loud confident shout, Jesus called, "Lazarus! Outside! *Come! Outside!*"

He waited. The silence could be felt. Then, from within the cave came the sound of a stirring. Tension gripped the watchers; John felt a cold fear crawling down his back. The sound grew louder, and fear disappeared with a mounting sense that God the Creator was greater than death, that with Jesus present anything was possible.

Not to their terror but to their joy they saw a figure shuffle out of the darkness. He came slowly into the sunshine, wrapped in graveclothes of unbleached linen, his head tied with the usual napkin. Yet there was a vigor and strength inside the bandages, a movement of muscle and limb which made John amazed that trappings of death should surround a Lazarus so obviously alive.

Disciples, sisters, mourners stood transfixed. Lazarus waited; for all his strength and health, he could not free his arms to release himself.

The voice of Jesus broke the tension. "Unbind him," he said, "and let him go home."

Then John knew that he did not dream, as Lazarus, Martha, and Mary fell joyfully into each other's arms.

Sixteen
THE LAST APPROACH

Those whose sorrow had turned joy at Lazarus' coming back to life returned to Bethany like their ancestors returning from exile: "When the Lord turned again the captivity of Zion, then were we like unto them that dream. Then was our mouth filled with laughter and our tongue with singing. The Lord hath done great things for us, whereof we are glad."

As the sisters served the feast which Martha had prepared for a wake, Lazarus' vitality showed the strength of the new life flowing through his veins; no one doubted that Jesus, invited to the seat of honor, had the power to raise the dead. Prominent Jews rose in their places to acknowledge that he was who he claimed to be; wherever he went they would follow.

John, however, noticed that several distinguished citizens

avoided the feast and saddled their donkeys. As he learned later, they rode as fast as the ascent would allow, then down into the Kidron ravine and up to the city, and did not dismount until they reached the palace of the high priest. Caiaphas was aghast at their eyewitness account. He summoned all Sanhedrin members at hand, including Nicodemus, a secret disciple of Jesus, who described it all to John afterward.

The deliberations were urgent and private, since formal meetings in the Hall of Polished Stones could convene only on certain days of the week. Jesus was a threat to their leadership. Opening the eyes of a man born blind was dangerous enough, but raising the dead would lead to a surge of popular support. Nicodemus heard his fellow members assess Jesus' motives and likely actions by their own. They convinced themselves that he would grasp at material power through a popular uprising against the occupying power, and as political realists they knew that this would fail. The furious Romans would destroy the Temple, remove the last vestiges of self-government, and crucify thousands of Jews.

The Sanhedrin debated what to do. Argument went round and round. Suddenly they heard the president's gavel.

Caiaphas spoke sharply and decisively. "You know nothing at all! It is much better that *one man should die* for the people instead of the whole nation perishing." He had a sound precedent in the case of a rebel against King David named Sheba. The royal troops were about to assault the town which sheltered him, and put its people to the sword, when the elders threw Sheba's head over the wall; the king's general lifted the seige and spared their lives. The Sanhedrin took Caiaphas' point. They began to discuss how to kill Jesus.

Nicodemus immediately sent a secret warning to Bethany. Jesus withdrew, first to an isolated village in the wild, rolling countryside some fifteen miles northeast of Jerusalem, alone with his disciples; then he crossed the Jordan to Herod's lands where the Sanhedrin's writ did not reach so effectively.

He resumed public teaching in the first days of spring, but his heart was in Jerusalem. When some Pharisees interrupted to say that Herod was out to kill him, Jesus refused to flee. He sent a message to "that fox" saying he would continue to work, "for surely no prophet can die outside Jerusalem." In tones of infinite sadness, he exclaimed: "O Jerusalem, Jerusalem, killing the prophets and stoning those who are sent to you! How often I have longed to gather your children together as a hen gathers her chicks under her wings, but you would not let me! Your house is forsaken. You will not see me again until you say, 'Blessed is he who comes in the name of the Lord.' "

Even as Jesus spoke, the scene was being set. Jews and proselytes were on their way by ship and caravan to reach Jerusalem for Passover. They came from Parthia and the Gulf and even a few from India; from Arabia and Ethiopia, from Spain and the far north African coasts; from Greece and Armenia; groups from all points of the compass took advantage of Roman peace and safe seas to converge on the Holy City. As the feast drew near, larger crowds from Galilee and every part of Palestine and Syria traveled the roads, until the 25,000 inhabitants of the city and suburbs were joined by at least 100,000 pilgrims. Whatever might happen to Jesus in Jerusalem would be reported throughout Palestine and in many parts of the world.

His relatives and friends from Galilee had started on the pilgrim route. At a camping place on the Great Road on the plateau beyond the Jordan, Jesus met his mother, and John and James met theirs. Mary and Salome brought other women who had looked after Jesus and his disciples during their earlier travels, including Joanna the wife of Chuza, Herod's steward, and Mary from Magdala, named by Christian tradition as the former prostitute who had poured the perfume on Jesus' head and had wiped his feet with her hair.

The Galileans comprised a large caravan of neighbors and strangers, including whole families. Word spread swiftly that Jesus of Nazareth had joined the travelers. Next morning, when they were striking their tents, John saw a young father shyly bring his small boy and ask Jesus to touch him for a blessing that would be a lifelong memory. Jesus put his hand on the child. Then other parents brought their children, including mothers with sleeping babies, until Jesus was the center of a nursery.

John, Peter, and several of the Twelve reacted sharply. Jesus had a long day's march ahead; he would want to teach the disciples as they walked, and all who gathered at the midday stop and the next resting place; he must not be jostled and fatigued by mere children. They began to shoo them away and rebuke the parents.

Jesus was indignant. "Let them come!" he ordered. "Do not hinder them!" He beckoned the children close and spoke to his disciples. "God's kingdom belongs to little ones like these," he said, a revolutionary idea, even to Peter and John who both loved children. "This is what I say to you: Anyone who will not receive the kingdom of God like a little child will never enter it." He took two of the smallest, one in each arm, and blessed them.

The disciples were abashed by the rebuke. But Jesus' indignation seemed honed to an even sharper edge by love for them no less than for the children, and John did not feel humiliated.

By now the caravan leaders had started the march. Families who had thronged round Jesus melted away with songs in their hearts. John brought Jesus his satchel and stick. Usually, Jesus not only had his own things ready but helped slow disciples get theirs; often he would have awakened them all with a cheerful word. This morning, however, the children had absorbed his attention.

Ready to start, Jesus stepped out and was about to get into his stride when a young man appeared; he wore a cloak of finest wool and a tunic of finest linen. His clothes were spotless despite the days on the journey; his fingers glittered with rings. Everything about him suggested new-made wealth and enterprise and authority.

He dropped to his knees and looked up anxiously. "Good Master," he said, "what must I do to obtain eternal life?"

Jesus turned the flattery. "Why do you call me good when no one is good except God alone?"

The young man did not answer.

"You know the Commandments," said Jesus, and ticked off five, all prohibitions: "Do not kill. Do not commit adultery. Do not steal. Do not bear false witness. Do not defraud." Then he added one out of sequence, most suitable for any young man who made money quickly: "Honor your father and mother!"

The rich man, still kneeling, answered that he had kept them all, since a boy. "What do I still miss; what must I do?" he urged.

A bystander who came from the same district murmured to John that the man had already built a synagogue, and thus had been elected a ruler despite his youth. Jesus was gazing at him, aware that he was so eager to do some great thing for his future, yet was blind to where his future lay. Suddenly Jesus bent forward, embraced him, and drew him up from his knees as if to call him to his side as he had called Matthew and Peter and John.

"One thing you miss," said Jesus. "If you want to be perfect, go away and sell everything you have and give to the poor—you will have treasure in heaven—and then *come, follow me.*"

The young man's face fell. He scratched his head. John could guess his thoughts. Gold and lands with their power and prestige and the means to do good as he wished would be out of his hands. Could he bear to strip himself of all he held dear?

The young man walked sadly away.

Jesus watched him, then turned to the disciples. "How hard it is for a rich man to enter the kingdom of God," he said.

John was amazed. Brought up to honor wealth as a sign of God's blessing, he could hardly believe his ears. It had been strange enough to learn that a little child may enter easily, but much more strange that a rich man could scarcely find the way. Jesus spoke again. "How hard it is, my children!" he said, and he used a well-known proverb to make his point. "It is easier for 'a camel to go through the eye of a needle' than for a rich man to enter heaven."

Peter muttered to John, "Who then can be saved?" Jesus directed at them all an intense gaze, until every eye focused upon him. He said, "This is impossible with man, but not with God. Everything is possible to God."

They started on the road again, settling into the steady pace which could be kept up mile after mile, but Peter would not drop the subject. After a while he said, "Look, we have left everything to follow you. What will there be for us?"

John shared Peter's feelings. But a shadow of grief passed over Jesus' face at their absorption in material reward. He stopped. John expected a rebuke. Instead, Jesus made a solemn pronouncement to the Twelve: "When all is made new and the Son of man sits on His throne of glory, you too will sit on twelve thrones, judging the twelve tribes.

"And there is nobody who has left home or brothers, or sisters or parents or children or friends for my sake and for the Good News, who will not receive much, much more in this life—houses, brothers, sisters, mothers and children and lands—and persecutions! And in the age to come, eternal life. But," he added, "many who are first shall be last, and the last first."

He walked on, and the Twelve closed up on him because he began a new story to show what the kingdom is like. As he talked, the spring flowers were showing, and they could see a field or two with the first shoots of barley, but he took their minds to hot days and the grape harvest, and told of a landowner who hired men early in the morning to work all day in his vineyard. They agreed on a denarius, a full day's fair wage. An hour or two later, he returned to the market-place and hired more men, saying, "I will pay you a fair wage."

As the day wore on and the landowner assessed his grape harvest, he hired others. An hour before dusk, back again, he saw men standing around. Jesus made the scene come alive: "The landowner asked them, 'Why do you stand here idle all day?' They said to him, 'Because no one has hired us.' He said to them, 'You go into the vineyard too.' " Dusk fell—work stopped. The men came for payment. The owner, in an unusual move, told his overseer to pay first the last men to be hired. They received a denarius. The first group therefore expected more, despite having agreed on a denarius; but he paid everybody the same.

The men grumbled loudly. "These men worked only an hour," complained their spokesman, "and you make them equal to us who have worked all day in the heat!"

"Friend," he replied, "I do you no wrong. Did you not agree on a denarius? Take what is yours and go. Cannot I do what I like with my own money? Are you envious because I am generous?"

Jesus summed up his story. "So you see, the last shall be first and the first last."

The disciples walked on in silence for a while, digesting this new approach to the rewards of service. But soon they were talking again, asking questions, listening to more stories. Unlike an official rabbi, whose disciples followed meekly behind, Jesus liked to keep his beside him. When they reached the next camping place, he again allowed all the pilgrims to gather round. That evening no disciple dared shoo away a child.

Next morning they turned west and began the descent to the Jordan crossing and Jericho. Every step brought them closer to Jerusalem.

Jesus walked ahead. John quickened pace, intending to fall in at his side. Then he saw Jesus' face and dropped back, and not one of the Twelve dared obtrude. John became amazed at the intensity of the suffering. In the past months they had all drawn so close to Jesus that his feelings invariably affected them. Even the women and the other disciples in the pilgrim caravan sensed the atmosphere and were afraid.

After a while Jesus stopped and took the Twelve a little aside from the road. He made them sit round as they often sat when he taught. John's heart went out to Jesus; he wanted to share the horror and lighten the load.

But when Jesus spoke, his first words suggested no horror at all, but glory. "We are going to Jerusalem," he began, "and all the prophecies about the Son of man must come true." John knew the prophets; they prophesied glory for the Messiah.

Jesus' next words shattered the vision. "The Son of man is going to be delivered up to the chief priests and scribes. They will condemn him to death. They will hand him to the Gentiles, and *they* will mock him, insult him, spit on him, flog him, kill him." (His phrases sounded like hammer on nails.) "He will be crucified—"

Peter did not interrupt. None of the disciples understood. Jesus was alive, vibrant, young, good. John could not imagine him put to the torture and dying as a criminal; he had escaped murderous attempts and would escape them again, whatever his fears.

"—And on the third day he will rise again." Jesus spoke the words without flourish as a statement of fact, but John, James, Peter, and all of them did not know what he was talking about, despite their vivid memory of Lazarus' tomb.

John closed his mind to thoughts of crucifixion. He dwelt on messianic glory. He recalled Jesus' earlier words about coming into the kingdom. When the march resumed, John drew James aside and they walked together, talking in whispers. Jesus would achieve power in the land soon. They must stake their claim. When the caravan stopped for the midday halt, and fires were being kindled and cooking pots filled, they sought out their mother and outlined their plan. A little later Salome approached Jesus with her sons at her side. She knelt to ask a favor.

Through her lips, in the presence of their ten colleagues, James and John begged Jesus to promise them the seats of authority and privilege immediately next to him, to the right and left of his throne.

"You do not know what you ask!" cried Jesus, addressing James and John. "Can you drink the cup I am going to drink? Be baptized with the baptism I am going to undergo?"

His strange language did not make them pause. They replied confidently, "We can."

"You *will* drink. You *will* be baptized. But it is not for me to grant these places—they belong to those for whom my Father has prepared them."

The other disciples descended on James and John in indignation.

Jesus called them all to himself without raising the voice which had stilled the waves and summoned from the grave: one firm word and the Twelve stood around sheepishly.

He laid down a new attitude to leadership. They were not to be lordly like earthly rulers. "Not so with you; anyone who is ambitious among you must become the servant of all. Whoever wants to be top must be your slave—just as the Son of man did not come to be waited upon but to serve and," he added, "to give his life as a ransom for many."

They walked on together. None of them saw his meaning. They thought he had spoken in a parable again and was leading them to his triumph.

Seventeen
ROYAL ENTRY

Jericho, with its fine houses and Herod's disused winter palace, looked lush with palms and gardens and shade trees. Southward, the Dead Sea glittered in the sunshine; to the west rose the bleak Judean mountains. Jesus and his disciples approached Jericho by the road which skirted ruins of earlier cities. The neighborhood had become a camping place for pilgrims and many joined him. By the time he reached the first houses, he was the focus of a spontaneous welcome, with townsfolk out on the streets to see Jesus of Nazareth passing by.

As the road crossed the stream which flowed into the palace garden, they heard a cry above the hubbub: "Jesus, Son of David, have mercy on me!" Spectators shouted, "Be quiet!" but the voice came again louder, joined soon by another. "Son of David have mercy on us!"

Jesus stopped. "Bring him," he ordered. The crowd fell

silent, and John heard someone at the roadside say, "Come on. Cheer up. He calls you."

The crowd parted, and John saw a blind beggar stand up and throw aside his cloak, a gesture of faith indeed, for he might not find it if he should return blind. Another blind beggar rose beside him, and willing hands guided them.

Jesus spoke with that tone of concern which John knew well. "What do you want me to do for you?" John reflected that it was a favorite phrase of his Master's, and never empty.

The beggars did not ask charity or a blessing. "Lord, we want to see," they said.

Jesus replied, "You *shall* see. Your faith has made you well."

He touched their eyes, and John was moved to the depths as he watched the impossible happen again. The two beggars blinked. They staggered a little, then leaped in the air with shouts of praise, which the crowd took up until the whole street echoed with the cry, "Hallelujah!"

The procession started again. The two men kept close to Jesus through Jericho and looked eagerly to left and right, shading their eyes in the sunlight, shouting their delight and their praise.

The triumphal walk was now well into the spacious new city, and the people lining the way stood thick on either side. Trees shaded the street, not in a formal avenue like a Roman highway but planted without design. Jesus passed into the shade of a sycamore-fig, an evergreen with short trunk and broad branches. Unexpectedly, he paused, looked up, and called out in a friendly tone, "Zaccheus! Come down quickly. I must stay at your house today!"

A face peered from the foliage. A stumpy little man scrambled down, his expensive clothes crumpled. He looked surprised, pleased, yet worried. Then he hurried ahead of the procession to make ready.

Townsfolk, on the contrary, looked dismayed. John overheard complaints and disbelief: "He is going to be the guest of a sinner!" John gathered that Zaccheus was taxgatherer for the Jericho district and, thus, in their opinion had insulted his name, which means "righteous." As chief collector of taxes, he held no official rank but had put in the highest bid and recruited subcollectors. The Romans required a heavy sum; the subcollectors wanted their share; his own wealth therefore depended on how much they could extort.

Among subject races of the empire, a rich taxgatherer like Zaccheus was even more of a pest than a tax collector like Matthew and doubly disgusting to Jews because wealth which was ill-gotten defiled all who it touched, except when received as charity. Therefore Zaccheus' company and delicacies were shunned by his neighbors. If he felt lonely, he had only himself to blame.

John knew this, and realized that Jesus had deftly faced the little man, who had climbed the tree to see him go by, with a choice: either to allow his guest to be defiled, or to purify his house by a true act of renunciation.

At length, Jesus, the disciples, and the crowd reached the elegant house on the outskirts of Jericho. John saw Zaccheus at the entrance with his family and household. Zaccheus bowed his welcome.

"Honorable Sir." He addressed Jesus in tones which all could hear. "Here and now I give half of all I possess to the poor." Since a formally expressed intention held almost legal force, no one doubted that he would carry it out, to disgorge his unfair gains and purify his house. He did more. "If I have cheated anybody of anything," he announced, "I will restore him four times the amount."

John noticed that Zaccheus had offered what the Law imposed on a rustler: restore four sheep for each one stolen. Jesus at once took up the allusion and addressed the crowd. "Today salvation has come to this home," he said. "And this man is a son of Abraham as much as you. For the Son of man came to seek and to save what is lost." John instantly recalled the parable. The Good Shepherd had found his lost sheep and brought him back to the fold. The ninety and nine must not shun him.

The Twelve enjoyed their stay. When they began the ascent to Jerusalem next morning, John and Peter shared with the others their pleasure that Jesus had called Zaccheus to be a disciple, because it disproved the strange talk about Jesus being crucified. There was no point in Jesus' calling disciples if he were about to die. Soon they were excitedly telling the Galilean pilgrims that God's kingdom was about to be revealed; Jesus would soon ascend the throne usurped by the Romans.

Jesus heard them. At the midday halt on the steep ascent, he told them a story about a nobleman who went away for a long time in order to receive a kingdom. Before leaving he distributed money to his servants to use on his behalf, and the parable turned on how faithfully and skillfully each discharged his trust before the king returned. Had the disciples ears to hear, this parable pointed them away from their excited expectations.

That evening they reached Bethany, shortly before the Sabbath began, and next day Bethany people joined together to provide a traditionally delightful Sabbath meal at the house of a neighbor known as Simon the Leper. Lazarus, strong and happy and a wonder to all, was an honored guest. Martha busied herself among the women who served. Mary, however, became again the center of an incident. This time it did not upset Martha but the Twelve.

Holding a pint-sized alabaster jar, Mary approached Jesus as he reclined at table. She broke the neck and poured a little on his head, then knelt and poured more over his feet. Fragrance filled the room and the house, stopping all conversation as guests and helpers recognized the scent of pure nard. This strong, delectable perfume came all the way from India, its cost reflecting the length of journey, yet Mary anointed Jesus with every drop in her jar and wiped his feet with her hair.

"What waste!" cried Judas Iscariot, the treasurer of the Twelve. "This cost a whole year's wages for a laborer. It should have been sold and the money given to the poor." The others agreed with Judas, though later, when he disclosed his true colors, they realized that he cared nothing for the poor and had pilfered the money box. They all began to rebuke Mary.

Jesus interrupted them. "Leave her alone. Why are you bothering her? She has done a beautiful thing to me. You will always have the poor and can help them whenever you wish, but you will not always have me. She has done what she could—*she has anointed my body for burial before the time.*"

A cold fear touched John's heart. Only a criminal's corpse could not be perfumed at burial. Foreboding silence closed John's ears to the prophecy which Jesus uttered: "Wherever the Good News is preached throughout the world, they will tell what she has done. She will never be forgotten."

John, however, forgot her soon enough in the exciting incidents which followed next afternoon. Jesus called John and James, and on his precise instructions they went up the hill to Bethphage, the neighboring village on the Mount of Olives. Exactly as Jesus had told them, they found a donkey tethered at a doorway, with a colt which had not been rid-den. They began to untie them. Some bystanders demanded to know why, but Jesus had provided what sounded like a password: "The Master wants them and will return them quickly."

Whoever the bystanders were (perhaps Jesus had arranged it at the Sabbath Feast and they were a fellow guest's servants) this sentence satisfied them.

John and James started down the hill leading the donkey, with her colt trotting contentedly behind, until they met Jesus and the rest of the Twelve as they walked slowly up.

Jesus surprised them all by indicating that he would not ride the donkey but the colt. John saw the significance at once. Jesus was about to enter Jerusalem. Pilgrims traditionally made their entrance to the Holy City on foot, but Jesus would ride, thus showing that he did not come as a pilgrim. Formal entrance to the Holy City riding a beast on which "no man had sat" was the prerogative of a king. And when the king came on a donkey, not on horseback, he came in peace. Matthew quickly recalled the prophecy in the Book of Zechariah: "Behold your king comes to you, humble and riding on an ass, on a colt the foal of an ass."

John and James had shed cloaks as they hurried. In a spontaneous gesture, they threw these over the colt to form a saddle, scarcely noticing that they thus covered the darker hair on spine and foreleg which forms the shape of a cross. Jesus mounted. Up to that moment, he and the Twelve had had the lane to themselves, but suddenly it filled with people. Citizens of Jerusalem came out by ancient tradition to welcome pilgrim caravans, but this greeting to Jesus had an excitement of its own. The sensation created by his raising Lazarus had not died down during the withdrawal across the Jordan, and when word came that Jesus would enter the city, groups hurried toward Bethany, where they missed him and came pouring up the lane.

They shouted their welcome and pulled off cloaks and laid them in the road. John led the colt the first few yards, but it did not shy at the noise, or rebel at its burden, and carried Jesus up the hill.

They entered Bethphage, a village set in fields and olive groves yet no rural backwater but a suburb of Jerusalem, filled already with Galilean pilgrims who streamed out to join the procession. They cut branches, especially palms, from the trees shading the lane and threw them ahead of the colt to form a carpet of greenery, or waved them as they walked. The palm branch was a symbol of victory. Some members of the procession sang the traditional welcome from one of the "Psalms of Ascent," with its invocation, "*Hosanna* (God, save us), *Hosanna,* blessed is he who comes in the name of the Lord." Others adapted words to praise Jesus and shouted, "Blessed is the King who comes in the name of the Lord! Peace in heaven and glory in the highest."

The procession reached the Roman road, already packed with pilgrims nearing Jerusalem. Seeing Jesus, many burst into songs of praise and joy and recalled his deeds in Galilee, until the Mount of Olives rang again. John thrilled to be part of a royal progress.

Shocked Pharisees shouted above the noise, "Teacher, rebuke your disciples!" Jesus had always rebuked attempts to make him a king. This time he called back, as he rode the symbol of peace and humility, "I tell you, if these stay silent, the very stones will cry out."

The brow of the hill had prevented more than a glimpse of the city, the palaces on Mount Zion and the walls, but as the road curled round the northern summit of the Mount of Olives to begin the descent, Jerusalem burst into view a mile to the west, soaring majestically from the Kidron abyss toward the blue sky. Once again John caught his breath at its perspective of beauty: the rock face, scattered with tombs and monuments, then the walls, then the bright stonework and marble of the Temple and the palaces, then the gold of pinnacles and towers glittering in the strong sunshine. Jerusalem was indeed "a city of great magnificence and mighty fame throughout the world," made yet more marvelous to John because he escorted his Master and beloved friend.

Suddenly Jesus gave a terrible cry. John swung round and saw the colt reined in, and Jesus weeping as he gazed at Jerusalem. "Oh, if you, even you," he shouted, "had only known, this very day, what would bring you peace! But it is hidden from your eyes."

He began to utter a terrifying prophecy, decribing Jerusalem, not as it now stood in its glory but as John would see it, to his horror, forty years on: the siege and the assault, the destruction and the fire, the thousand or more naked men nailed to crosses, while starving women and children were driven into slavery as the Romans rewarded rebellion and prolonged resistance. "They will not leave one stone upon another," Jesus mourned, "because you did not recognize the time when God came to save you!"

He touched his mount. All moved on.

They resumed their song. At the foot of the Mount of Olives, the stream of pilgrims merged with others from Emmaus and the north, and they pressed on together toward the northern gate which led to the city streets, with the Temple soaring above. Before they could reach the gate, a crowd poured out from within. By that instinct which sweeps an eastern city, hundreds had rushed to see Jesus enter. Pilgrims caught the excitement and inquired who came; Galileans already arrived gave the answer with pride:

"It is Jesus, the prophet from Galilee." Judeans and pilgrims and Galileans struggled for a place as the procession neared the gate, with Jesus riding at the center of an adoring, vocal, palm-waving mob.

Roman sentries looked down from the walls on the seething mass. At Passover the garrison stayed on full alert, but none saw cause for alarm, for the noise and crowds were normal when half the world's Jews squeezed themselves into Jerusalem, as it seemed to a scoffing sentry. But Pharisees despaired. "What shall we do? The whole world has gone after him."

Eighteen

COURTS
OF THE TEMPLE

Next morning John was again approaching Jerusalem with Jesus, who this time was on foot, without a crowd.

The previous evening had perplexed the Twelve. After his deliberately royal entry, Jesus had not exploited the mood of the hour. He had not tried to seize political power or fan religious fervor. He sent the donkeys back to their owner, allowed the mob to fade away, entered the Temple, and saw what needed to be done; then, before darkness, he had gone quietly home to Bethany. In the morning, as Jesus led the way down the Mount of Olives by the steep path which he had avoided with the donkeys, and into the Kidron Valley, John wondered what Jesus had in mind.

They climbed out of the valley. As they neared the Shushan or Beautiful Gate of the Temple, they heard the bleating of lambs, lowing of cattle, and the cries of traders.

Emerging from the gate into the vast Court of the Gentiles, they were confronted by the roar of an oriental market: a desecration which Caiaphas in his greed had established three years earlier, shortly before John had come to Jerusalem with Jesus after the wedding in Cana. He could vividly recall Jesus pulling out strands of his headdress to make a whip and driving out the cattle and sheep. His gesture had infuriated the authorities, who had allowed the commerce to resume.

Jesus now stood surveying the scene. Under the colonnades round the court sat money changers, since pilgrims must pay the Temple tax in a particular coinage. The open area, wide and long, was almost filled with flocks and herds, for during the seven days of the feast each worshiper must sacrifice 14 bullocks, 7 goats and rams, and 49 lambs: at the last Passover before the siege by the Romans more than 255,000 lambs would be slaughtered. Few pilgrims brought their own beasts, but the proper place for the market was the slope of the Mount of Olives and not the Court of the Gentiles; John saw Gentile "God-fearers," forbidden on pain of death to enter the inner courts, trying to pray amid the din.

Jesus watched and listened for a few moments. Then he filled his lungs, and in a voice which carried above the bleating and lowing, shouts of sellers, and arguments of the cheated, he called out texts from the prophets Isaiah and Jeremiah: "It is written: 'My house shall be called a house of prayer for all nations.' But you are making it 'a den of robbers'!"

With set face, he walked up to the nearest row of moneychangers' tables and pushed them over, one after another. Coins clattered on the paving stones and rolled away. He upset the seats of the sellers of doves and drove flocks and herds toward the gate, calling out repeatedly the texts by which buying and selling in the Temple stood condemned. This time he made no whip. His righteous indignation was enough, backed by his reputation and the guilty consciences of merchants and customers, and the panic which swept through the crowd.

As the Twelve helped Jesus, John was impressed beyond all else by the expression on his face: not of moral force only but of love. John could feel the love which drove Jesus: love for God and his Temple, love for the cheated, love for the merchants and herdsmen who had been trapped into sacrilege by greed and custom, even love for the Temple authorities who had betrayed their trust. These were too amazed to intervene.

The Court of the Gentiles was emptying rapidly, leaving offal, spilled coins, and overturned tables. Jesus moved to the gate which led from the city. He stopped the flow of men and women who flagrantly used the Temple area as a short-cut to the markets. Priests and Temple police could hardly object to his upholding their own regulations. The court was now becoming quiet.

Suddenly John, recovering his breath, heard a different sound—a tap-tap of sticks, a shuffling of crippled feet. The blind and the lame were entering the Temple to find Jesus, and now John saw Pharisees throw up their hands in horror: they had ruled that the blind and the lame were excluded from appearing before the Lord in his Temple, and from offering sacrifices, though a few sat begging at the inner gates. Jesus, however, at once welcomed these outcasts and began to heal, so that lame men leaped and blind men saw.

Then came the boys and girls, an unforgettably touching sight, especially to Peter. They poured into the Temple despite being ritually excluded on grounds of decorum, and danced around Jesus. *"Hosanna,* God save the Son of David," they shouted, until chief priests and scribes were beside themselves. Commerce and shortcuts could be winked at, but for children to shout in the sacred courts affronted sanctity. Moreover their shouts acclaimed Jesus as King of the Jews. The officials were appalled. They rushed toward Jesus. "Do you hear what these children are saying?"

"Yes," replied Jesus. "And do you not know the Scripture: 'From the lips of children and babes at the breast, you have brought perfect praise'?"

To John his words sounded less a retort than an appeal in sorrow, not anger; as if he pleaded once more that the religious leaders should open their eyes to the truth.

They did not respond. He thanked the children and healed remaining cripples, then turned his back on his opponents and left the Temple.

Twenty-four hours later, on Tuesday morning, the Twelve again followed Jesus down the Mount of Olives, walking through the Garden of Gethsemane and across the Kidron and up under the cream-colored walls until they entered the Temple once more, to find that the flocks, herds, and money changers had not returned to the Court of the Gentiles.

Many people noticed Jesus' arrival and gathered round him, but before he could reach a shady portico from which to teach, he was stopped by a knot of chief priests, scribes, and Sanhedrin members, flanked by a few Temple guards, who evidently had awaited his appearance.

They demanded to know who had given him authority for his actions of the previous day. Their question held menace, since unauthorized behavior within the Temple precincts could be punished, and the guards might hurry Jesus away to be beaten.

He did not flinch. Nor did he answer. Instead he threw a

question back. "The baptism of John: was it from heaven or men? Answer me that, and I will tell you my authority to do these things."

The question put them on the horns of a dilemma. They withdrew to argue the point while Jesus waited and the crowd relished the officials' embarrassment, for if they acknowledged that the Baptist's authority had been from heaven, they would have answered their own question: John the Baptist had hailed Jesus as Son of God and as Messiah or Christ, and Messiah could do as he wished in his Temple. "But," muttered the rulers, "if we say, 'From man,' the people will stone us. Everybody holds that John was a true prophet."

At last the rulers said shamefacedly, "We do not know."

"Then I will not answer your question either," replied Jesus. "I will not tell you what is my authority."

The crowd knew it instinctively. While the rulers' representatives retired to plot his downfall, the people settled down to listen. That day and the next Jesus sat for hours teaching. He was not addressing a multitude as in Galilee, when his voice had carried far and clear across a hillside or beach. He spoke intimately. The Twelve and the other disciples who had traveled with him, or had come to his side in Judea, listened in the shade of the columns—along with his mother and the other Mary, Martha, and Lazarus, Salome, and many whose names were never known to posterity.

Behind them, under the sunshine or the passing afternoon clouds, stood an ever-changing audience—pilgrims, citizens, priests, Levites—stopping a while on their way to or from the sacrifices or rituals in the inner courts. Some stayed until the shadows lengthened, others wandered off, busy with Temple duties or preparations for the feast.

He spoke frankly about the faithlessness and hypocrisy of

the religious leaders and the coming fate of the nation. He drove home his warnings by telling vivid stories, such as his parable of the vineyard let out to tenants who not only refused the owner his share of the grape harvest but maltreated or even killed his collectors. Finally, he sent his only and dearly loved son, expecting them to respect him. Instead, they threw him out and killed him, "that his inheritance may be ours." As he listened, John knew that if the owner had no heir and took no action, the vineyard might legally lapse to the tenants; but he was not surprised at the reaction of the audience when Jesus put the question: "When the owner comes, what will he do to those tenants?"

"He will put them to death and let out the vineyard to others, who will give him his share at harvest."

Jesus looked squarely at them, and with an apt quote he warned solemnly that God would take away the kingdom from the Jewish nation and give it to others.

This was reported to the chief priests, who angrily resented such an attack. Soon a posse of Temple guards clanked up to the fringe of the crowd as if to break it up and arrest him. They saw that the people hung on his words. Under orders not to risk a riot, they withdrew.

Then Jesus told a story of a king who had prepared a banquet to celebrate his son's wedding, but the important guests sent excuses, or beat up or killed his messengers. Therefore, the king ordered his army to punish them, and sent servants into the streets and lanes to bring in the poor, the lame, and the blind, both bad and good. Still there were empty places. "Go into the highways and hedges," he ordered, "and compel them to come in so that my house is full. None of those who were first invited shall taste my banquet."

As he continued his teaching, the audience grew larger,

spreading into the area which previously had been cluttered by sheep pens. Then John saw one section draw back to let through a little procession of somewhat supercilious young men—students of a theology school, mixed with officers of Herod's army. They walked up to Jesus. One of them cleared his throat, and with little attempt to disguise insincerity, he poured out compliments: "Teacher, we know you are a man of integrity. You teach God's way in truth. You are not influenced by men, because you do not care who they are. Tell us your opinion: Is it right to pay taxes to Caesar or not?"

John held his breath. It seemed that now Jesus was impaled on the horns of a dilemma. If he said yes, he would be a collaborator. If he said no, the Pharisees who had sent the students and officers could denounce him to the Romans, who cared nothing for Jewish arguments, but would crucify a man for sedition. John could see no way out.

Without a pause Jesus replied: "Hypocrites! Why try to trap me? Show me a coin used to pay the tax."

A young man produced a coin. "Whose likeness and inscription is this?"

"Caesar's."

"Give to Caesar what is Caesar's and to God what is God's!"

The young men were amazed and abashed, and went away. Jesus' answer would be dissected, interpreted, expounded, and quoted without end, but the immediate effect was to spring the trap.

Opponents returned again and again. John found himself a listener at a great debate. On the one side he heard wily lawyers and scribes, self-important Pharisees in white robes, politically minded Sadducees, and students eager to prove zeal and verbal skill. On the other side sat Jesus, thirty-three years old, clear-eyed, holding himself well so that he was a delight to watch and hear, yet without pomposity, arrogance, or malice as he countered their thrusts.

They seemed determined to destroy him. Jesus might speak truth, but he looked frail against the weight of official opposition. John knew that the Sanhedrin itself numbered believers in Jesus who kept silent because of fear of the Pharisees. If they had ways to compel powerful men to keep silent, they could find means to silence Jesus forever.

Jesus appeared to ignore his danger, indeed to court it. He continued to state his claims without compromise; he did not hesitate to denounce the religious leaders in plain terms and thus to increase their fury.

Events mounted toward a climax. Huge, excitable crowds filled the city and the Temple. While Jesus taught, John heard the sound of Roman trumpets from the Fortress of Antonia which dominated the Temple from the northwest, and knew that Pontius Pilate, the Roman Governor, had arrived from Caesarea; he always took up residence during Passover, in case of trouble. Herod the Tetrarch was already at his own palace, but the two were not on speaking terms.

John felt the pressure of forces greater than he saw; he drew strength from Jesus' serenity but could not escape the sense of menace hanging over his head.

John did not understand what was happening, but a clue came when Peter tugged at his robe and pointed to Andrew and Philip escorting some Greeks through the crowd to meet Jesus. Afterward, John learned that the men had approached Andrew, who like Peter and Philip had been born in a Gentile city, and said they would like to see Jesus. Andrew, worried lest Jesus might dislike talking to Gentiles in the Temple, consulted Philip; then together they introduced the foreigners to Jesus.

With Greeks from a distant land standing before him, Jesus made a solemn pronouncement:

"The hour is come" he proclaimed, "for the Son of man to be glorified! Unless a grain of wheat falls to the ground and dies, it remains alone. If it dies, it bears much fruit."

He expounded the theme a little and then said: "Now my soul is troubled. And what shall I say, 'Father, save me from this hour'? No, it was for this very reason that I came to this hour."

Then he lifted his eyes and voice to heaven and said loudly: "Father, glorify your name!"

A sound like thunder reverberated round the court, though the sky was clear: "I have glorified it and will glorify it again."

John, Peter, and James all heard the voice, like the voice they had heard on Mount Hermon. The people said it was thunder.

Jesus spoke again: "That voice was for your sakes, not mine. Now comes judgment on this world; now the ruler of this world will be driven out."

His gaze held both Jews and Greeks. "And I, when I am lifted up from the earth, will draw all men to me."

John's heart chilled as he recalled Jesus' earlier words to the Twelve: "The Son of man will be crucified."

Nineteen
THE UPPER ROOM

Jesus had finished teaching on Wednesday afternoon and had walked up the steps into the court where only Jews might go: the Court of the Women. Ahead, the Levites were singing at the farther entrance leading to the Court of the Priests, which contained the altar and the slaughtering slabs. Beyond rose the towering marble building of the Holy Place, where the great curtain or veil of the Temple shut off the Holy of Holies, except to the high priest once a year.

Jesus sat down near the Treasury and watched as worshipers threw in coins. He saw a richly clad merchant shake a fat bag of gold into one of the trumpet-shaped offertory boxes. A pompous Pharisee strode up and looked around to make sure that someone saw how much he put in. Pilgrims passed by, casually throwing in coins, while several citizens looked resentful as they fulfilled their obligations. Then a little old woman, coarsely dressed in widow's weeds, hobbled up to a box. She stood a moment and bowed her head in prayer, with an expression on her face of devotion and pleasure. She fumbled for her purse and shook it into her hand.

All that fell out were two small bronze coins, the lowest in the Jewish currency, together equal to a quarter of a Roman copper. She took the two coins and reverently dropped them into the box and walked off with a light step, oblivious to being observed.

Jesus called the disciples' attention to the woman. "That poor widow," he said delightedly, "put more into the Treasury than all the others! They gave something out of their wealth, but she, out of her poverty, put in everything—all she had to live on."

He stood up and began to lead them out of the Temple, but the disciples were in a sightseeing mood and pointed out to Jesus the great stones of the buildings, some adorned with precious stones; and the magnificence of the pillars and arches, the stairways, and the gates of gold and pearl.

Jesus looked grave. "Do you see all these great buildings? The time is coming when not one stone will be left on another. All will be thrown down."

He remained solemn as they descended into the Kidron Valley and climbed the path up the Mount of Olives to his favorite place of prayer, the Garden of Gethsemane. He sat down and looked back over the city and his eyes filled with tears. John and James and Peter and Andrew talked softly among themselves, then went up to him. "Tell us, when will it all happen?"

In reply, Jesus began to prophesy at length, and they tried to understand. Sometimes he was describing in detail the terrible events of the coming Jewish War and the fall of

Jerusalem. He talked too of even greater sufferings throughout the world which would be the prelude to his return in
glory. As John listened, his mind's eye seemed to see in one
view two vivid pictures of different historic climaxes, one
behind the other, without being granted a clue to the length
of time between. "Be ready, be on your watch," Jesus urged
repeatedly. He warned them by straight talk and by parable
how to prepare and to endure, and how to avoid being
deceived.

John had listened in the synagogue to rabbis discoursing
on the end of the age: the prospect of world tribulation and
a final judgment was not strange to any of the Twelve, but
Jesus spoke differently from a rabbi, because he centered all
on himself, the Son of man. He painted history as moving
toward his own return in glory. Though the Father alone
knew the day or the hour, they must never doubt that it
would happen. Heaven and earth would pass away, "but my
words will not pass away."

He ended on a characteristic note. The evening shadows
were already falling across the city, which stood out in sil-
houette against the setting sun, when he told them one more
parable. He likened the people of all nations to sheep and
goats as they assembled before his throne for the last judgment. In Palestine their fleeces are superficially similar. Like
a shepherd the king separates them, the sheep on his right,
the goats on his left. The "sheep" are welcomed to their
eternal inheritance: "For I was hungry and you gave me
food; I was thirsty and you gave me drink; I was a stranger
and you took me in; naked and you clothed me; I was sick
and you visited me, in prison and you came to me."

The "sheep" are puzzled and ask, "When?" And the king
answers, "When you did it to one of the least of these my
brothers, you did it to me."

Then the king sentences the "goats" to punishment, "for I was hungry and you gave me no food, thirsty and you gave me no drink. . . . " The "goats" cannot remember starving the king or leaving him thirsty or naked or sick or in prison. But the king rejects the excuse: "Because you did nothing for one of the least of my brothers, you did nothing for me."

While the Twelve silently absorbed his parable, Jesus said quietly, "As you know, the Passover is two days away, and the Son of man will be handed over to be crucified."

He led his men back through the shadows to Bethany. They walked in silence, under the Passover moon, two days off the full; a cold fear, mixed with disbelief, clutched at John.

John slept fitfully that last night they would spend in Bethany—for the Passover night must be spent within the city walls. John feared for Jesus' safety and was relieved in the morning when Peter showed him two short swords. He was even more relieved that Jesus did not lead the Twelve back to Jerusalem but rose early and went to spend the morning alone in the garden on the Mount of Olives, hiding himself from listeners and opponents. The Twelve sat out of earshot, though Peter and John made sure that they could see him and be ready to spring to his protection. Away from the city, they felt he was safe; for though the authorities were unwilling to risk a riot by arresting him in the Temple, Jerusalem offered opportunities to murderers.

Judas Iscariot, as treasurer and administrator for the Twelve, left them soon afterward to buy their Passover lamb; every household or company of pilgrims must sacrifice and eat a living male, less than a year old. Time passed, and John wondered vaguely why Judas took so long, but suspected nothing.

Unknown to John, Judas made a detour on his way to the

sheep market, to the high priest's palace. He approached furtively, then disclosed himself as an informer on Jesus of Nazareth, and was admitted at once: an informer was the chief priests' one hope of seizing Jesus without a riot.

Judas asked, "What will you give me if I betray him to you?" Judas had priced Mary of Bethany's nard at 300 small silver coins of the Romans. In the high priest's palace, they used a larger Greek coin worth three of these. They counted out thirty, less than a third of the value of Mary's nard. For these thirty pieces of silver, he promised to hand over Jesus quietly.

Every age has pondered the motive. John believed that Satan entered Judas Iscariot's soul. The most popular conjectures other than greed or jealousy are disappointment that Jesus refused to launch a rebellion; or a belief that if Jesus were arrested he would summon heavenly hosts to his rescue and precipitate his kingdom on earth.

Leaving the palace, Judas bought a lamb and carried it back to Bethany, where like thousands of other lambs in Jerusalem and the suburbs it spent the hours tethered in the shade within reach of grass or hay and water, not suspecting that its blood must be spilled at twilight. Judas joined his equally unsuspecting friends.

Early in the afternoon they all approached Jesus to ask where to prepare the Passover feast. Judas stood close, listening intently, but Jesus did not answer the question directly. He gave detailed instructions to John and Peter which, as they realized afterward, could provide no clue to Judas: Jesus did not want any interruption at his last supper with the Twelve.

They hurried away, fetched the lamb, and carried it to Jerusalem. As they entered they saw, exactly as Jesus had told them, a man marked out from the crowd by an earthenware water jar on his shoulder: women carried these; men carried wineskins. He led them silently through the streets and the partially filled ravine which split Jerusalem, and ascended to the upper city at the southwestern corner. John could see the Temple below to the east and Herod's palace to the west. The water carrier stopped at a substantial house.

They were greeted by the father or guardian of young John Mark, the future companion of Barnabas and Paul. Peter said, as instructed, "The Master asks, 'Where is my guest room where I may eat the Passover with my disciples?'" The host bowed, and escorted them, not to the common guest area but upstairs to a large room, quiet and already furnished with cushions and a low table.

Then they took the lamb to the Temple and joined the companies waiting their turn at the altars.

The great gates opened to the inner court. As they entered, John heard Levites chant and trumpets blow, while the fires and the smell of blood drove home to him again the age-old teaching that the sacrifice of an innocent on his behalf was the price of his eternal safety. When their turn came, John held the lamb while a white-robed priest held a golden bowl and caught the blood as Peter cut its throat. The bowl passed from priest to priest until the last of the line threw the blood at the altar's base.

Expert hands skinned the slain lamb as it lay on a rough frame between the shoulders of Peter and John; they removed the innards to burn them, taking care that not one bone should be broken. The disciples left the Temple to the sounds of trumpets, singing, and the bleat of lambs awaiting slaughter, and carried the carcass back to the home of John Mark. Rhoda the maid had an oven ready to roast it while they laid the table with bitter herbs and sauce, wine, unleavened bread, plus other requirements of a Passover feast.

Toward evening, shortly before the Passover began at 6 P.M., they heard Jesus and his ten other disciples ascending the stairs to the upper room. John gave him the kiss of peace with special affection, born of relief that he had passed through the city safely. Judas Iscariot, not knowing their destination, had not earned his thirty pieces of silver, and the unsuspecting John greeted him with the same warmth as he did the other disciples.

John had placed thirteen cushions in a horseshoe round the low table: three at the top, five on each side, leaving the bottom open for service. At Passover everyone must recline, not sit. Jesus took the head of household's place at the top, leaning on his left elbow in the normal way with feet stretched away from the table and his right hand free for food. John reclined on Jesus' right, immediately below him. Peter took the bottom of the table to his left, ready to fetch the roast lamb at the correct moment, but Judas hurried to the top to the other cushion next to Jesus—the chief guest's place (the guest reclining on the host's left must look down on him) which Judas regarded as the treasurer's privilege. A quarrel blew up later over precedence, but Jesus stopped it.

As they took their places, Jesus looked around at these special friends. "Oh," he cried, "how much I have longed to eat this Passover with you before I suffer, for I tell you I shall never eat it again until it is fulfilled in the kingdom of God." John did not understand.

Jesus stood up and began the supper by the time-honored ceremony of giving thanks over the first of four cups in front of him: "Blessed are you, Lord our God, King of the world, who created the fruit of the vine." The opening words of the Passover liturgy were familiar; but when he handed the cup to be shared round, and resumed his couch, he broke the familiar silence. "I shall never drink of the fruit of the

vine again," he said, "until the kingdom of God comes."
John still did not understand.

Before eating, the head of the household or company must
ceremonially wash his hands. Jesus again rose from his place,
but he did not place his hands in the basin. Instead, he
removed his robe. John watched perplexed as Jesus pulled
off his sleeveless tunic, woven from top to bottom without
seam, and stood before them stripped to his loincloth like a
slave. John never forgot the love and tenderness, the serenity
on Jesus' face as he wound a towel round his waist, took the
basin, and knelt down to wash Judas' feet. He wiped them
with the towel, then moved to the next. Disciples watched in
total silence as their Master worked as if he were their lowest
slave.

When he came to Peter, Peter said in astonishment,
"Lord, are you going to wash my feet?"

"You do not know what I am doing to you now. You will
understand later."

Peter looked genuinely shocked and drew his feet back.
"You shall never wash my feet!"

"If I do not wash you, you are saying in effect that you are
not my follower."

"Then, Lord, not just my feet but my hands and my
head."

Jesus shook his head. He reminded the Twelve that when
a man comes home from the baths he needs only to wash his
feet. "And you are clean—but not all of you," he said as he
dried Peter's feet.

John's feet were the last to be washed. John accepted the
honor humbly and gratefully. Jesus put on his tunic and robe
and reclined again on his cushion while Peter fetched the
dish of lamb.

While they ate, Jesus taught them. The meat had been

roasted enough to be easily handled, and they had segments of unleavened bread to sop up the gravy, They gave undivided attention to Jesus' words. He said: "I gave you an example. If I, your Master and Lord, washed your feet, you should wash each other's feet."

As the meal proceeded, Jesus followed the ancient Passover liturgy yet changed it by actions and words which sank deep into the consciousness, though neither John nor others yet understood. When Jesus rose, took bread, gave thanks, and broke it, he passed the pieces to them. "Take and eat. This is my body broken for you. Do this in remembrance of me."

When he lifted another of the cups of wine and spoke the words of thanks, he handed it to them. "Drink it, all of you. This is my blood of the new covenant which is poured out for you and for many for the forgiveness of sins."

Judas took the bread and sipped the wine with the others. Suddenly John saw their Master deeply troubled, just as he had been before the tomb of Lazarus. Jesus quoted from a psalm of David, "He who shares my bread has lifted up his heel against me." With great emphasis he declared, "One of you is going to betray me!"

John, horrified, stared at any disciple he could see. Jesus impressed upon them again that a betrayer sat in their midst. They became very sad and, not realizing that he referred to events that very night, they all searched their hearts whether they could ever betray. "Lord, is it I?" John asked, as the same anxious question came from almost every couch.

Peter caught John's eye and beckoned him to beg Jesus to name the traitor. John carefully did so without attracting attention, by leaning closer against Jesus' chest without changing position. Jesus replied in a murmur, "It is he to whom I give this morsel when I have dipped it."

He stretched to dip a piece of food in the bowl of sauce. He offered it to Judas, a gesture of honor which opened a last route of repentance. Judas hesitated, muttering, "Is it I, Rabbi?" He could have stepped back from the brink, thrown himself on his knees, flung away the thirty pieces of silver secreted on his person, and confessed what Jesus already knew.

The moment passed; Judas took the morsel.

"Do it more quickly," said Jesus softly. Judas rose from his couch and walked from the room. John had a sudden urge to stop or denounce him, or rush to one of the two swords; but without Jesus' orders he did nothing. The rest thought Judas had been sent on some errand as treasurer.

Judas descended the stairs and went out into the night.

Twenty
THE GARDEN

With Judas gone, the atmosphere in the Upper Room became more intimate but not more relaxed. Jesus, still reclining at table, said immediately, "Now the Son of man is glorified, and God is glorified in him." John had looked forward eagerly to the glory of his Master all the time they had walked together toward Jerusalem. At last it would happen.

But Jesus dashed high expectations. He threw all eleven disciples into alarm with his next words. "Little children"—he had never called them "little children" before—"I will be with you only a little longer. You will look for me, but I tell you now what I told the Jews. Where I am going you cannot come."

John was horrified. He looked down the table to Peter and saw him shocked and dismayed, and he heard an anguished murmur from every couch. Before they could voice their protests, Jesus rose from his place. The head of a family or company usually addressed them at the close of the Passover feast, with questions interjected by his listeners. He began: "I give you a new commandment, *Love one another*. You must love one another just as I have loved you. That is how all men will know that you are my disciples, because you love one another."

John had heard rabbis and Jesus himself extol the great commandments, to love God and one's neighbor, and to love each other as intimate brothers, in the same selfless way in which Jesus had loved them; this would be a test indeed. Jesus, however, did not expound the theme because Peter interrupted. His mind was not on brotherly love.

"Lord," he demanded, "where are you going?"

Jesus repeated, "I am going where you cannot follow now. But you will follow later."

"Lord, why can't I follow you now? I will 'lay down my life' for you." John detected an echo of Jesus' story of the Good Shepherd.

Jesus looked at him. "Will you lay down your life for me? Believe me. Before the cock crows, you will deny me three times."

Jesus spoke to calm them. "Don't let your hearts be troubled. Trust in God; trust in me too." He was going to the Father's house to prepare them a room, and would return and take them there himself, to be with him. "You know where I am going, and you know the way."

Thomas interrupted. "Lord, we do not know where you are going, so how can we know the way?"

Jesus replied in clear, simple, unmistakable words which, in the years to come, John loved to ponder over and over again. "I am the way and the truth and the life," said Jesus.

"No one comes to the Father except through me. If you really knew me, you would know my Father too. And from now on you do know him, for you have seen him."

Philip suddenly voiced the idea that was in the back of all their minds. "Show us the Father! And that will be enough for us."

"Have I been with you all this time, Philip," Jesus answered, "and you do not know me? Anyone who has seen me has seen the Father. How can you say, 'Show us the Father?'" And Jesus pressed this home.

The Master reclined again on his couch, and all that he taught for the remainder of the evening had an unforgettable intimacy. Much of it John did not fully grasp at the time, partly because he could not realize that Jesus' crucifixion was less than twelve hours away, and partly because Jesus spoke prophetically about the future.

Listening carefully, John heard Jesus give a promise which seemed almost too good to be real: that when he went away he would ask the Father and the Father would send Someone to be with them always as counselor and comforter, the Spirit of truth, who would be none other than Jesus himself, but not in physical form. "I will not leave you as orphans. I will come to you. Before long, the world will see me no more but you will see me. Because I live, you also will live. On that day you will realize that I am in my Father, and you are in me, and I in you." He calmed their fears. "I leave you peace," he said. "It is my peace that I give you—the peace the world cannot give. Do not let your hearts be troubled. Do not be afraid."

At last Jesus told them that they must leave the Upper Room for what was coming, and as they rose from their couches he called them, with deep affection, "those who stood by me in my trials." He promised them special places and special work in his kingdom. Then he looked at Peter. "Simon, Simon," he said, not using the nickname "Rock," "Satan wants to sift you like wheat. But I have prayed for *you* that your faith may not fail. And when you have turned back to me, strengthen your brothers!"

Peter insisted: "Lord, I am ready to go to prison with you, and to death."

Jesus again warned solemnly that Simon Peter would disown and deny him before cockcrow.

He asked them all whether they had lacked anything when sent out on their own without purse or satchel or sandals.

"Nothing," they all exclaimed.

"But now, take a purse if you have it, and a satchel. If you have not got a sword, sell your coat and buy one!"

They showed him the two swords (common to be worn in the Roman world) which Peter and another disciple had unbuckled on entering the room. He said, "That is enough." But before they could understand what he had meant earlier about the swords, he froze their hearts by saying that a particular prophecy about himself must be fulfilled, "He shared the fate of criminals." John knew the quotation at once, from Isaiah's prophecy of the Suffering Servant: "He willingly gave his life. He shared the fate of criminals. He took the place of many sinners."

By now it was late at night. Led by Jesus, they sang the final psalm of the Passover liturgy, then went downstairs. John caught a glimpse of young John Mark, woken by their song, peeping from behind the curtain drawn across his sleeping place.

Jesus and his disciples walked quietly through the city in the light of the nearly full moon. As they passed the Temple's closed gates with the symbolic golden vine, Jesus taught them that they were like the branches and he the vine; they could do nothing cut away from him, but would bear much fruit if they remained part of him. He taught about God's love; and he said, "Greater love has no man than this, that he lay down his life for his friends. You are my friends if you do whatever I command you."

Grief began to overwhelm them as they walked. He told them that the world would be gleeful at his death while they mourned and wept. "But your grief will turn to joy! Now is your time of grief, but I will see you again; and you will rejoice and no one will take away your joy." John heard him again promising to come back, but in their sorrow none of them could grasp his promise.

By now they were looking over the Kidron ravine in the high moon near midnight. All households and pilgrim companies were still at Passover feasts, or asleep, and the city was still. Perhaps the cool air sharpened wits, for as he continued to teach, his words suddenly seemed startlingly clear. "I came from the Father and entered the world. Now I am leaving the world and am going back to the Father."

They all spoke at once. "You are speaking clearly! And not in parables. . . . We can see now—you know all things. . . . We believe that you came from God."

"Do you believe? A time is coming—it has come now— when you will all be scattered, each to his own home. You will all fall away. It is written, 'I will strike the shepherd and the sheep will be scattered.' You will leave me alone. Yet I am not alone, for my Father is with me."

Jesus said again, "You will all fall away, but," he added, "after I have risen, I will go ahead of you into Galilee."

At that, Peter repeated his earlier boast. "I will never deny you! If everyone does, I will not! I'll go to prison, to judgment for your sake."

"Truly, truly, Peter," repeated Jesus sadly, "this very night before the cock crows twice, you will deny me three times."

But Peter insisted vehemently, "If I have to die with you, I will not deny you." John echoed his words, and so did they all.

They walked on a little, then Jesus stopped. He waited until everyone was close to him and said: "I have told you these things so that in me you may have peace. In the world you will have trouble. But take heart! I have overcome the world."

As they stood around, he looked toward heaven and began to pray. "Father, the hour is come. Glorify your Son that your Son may glorify you. . . . The disciples lifted their hearts in prayer with him, awed by the intimacy with which he prayed for them and for all who would believe through them.

The prayer was long, but John did not notice the coldness of the night, for Jesus took them right into the warmth of God's presence. Jesus ended: "Righteous Father, though the world does not know you, I know you; and they know that you have sent me. I have made you known to them, and will continue to make you known in order that the love you have for me may be in them, and that I myself may be in them."

No one spoke as the disciples followed Jesus across the Kidron ravine to the Mount of Olives. They climbed a little way up the steep lane and turned into the olive Garden of Gethsemane, where he had often taken them. When they reached the stone shelter housing the oil press which gave the garden its name, he told them to sit down "while I go over there and pray." He beckoned Peter, James, and John to come.

As they walked beside him in the bright moonlight, John was appalled to see Jesus shuddering, in an anguish more intense than John believed to be possible. "My soul is crushed with sorrow, almost to the point of death. Stop here," he said, "and keep awake."

He went a stone's throw farther and fell to the ground, and John heard his agonized prayer. "*Abba,* Father," he cried, using that intimate term which John would never have dared use himself. He saw him kneeling against a stone, his head uplifted to heaven, his arms stretched out, his whole body convulsed.

The hour was late; they were exhausted, weighed down with sorrow. Peter took refuge in sleep, then James, then John.

A secret eyewitness and eavesdropper stayed awake: Mark, the valiant young man in the first flush of his strength, who had risen from bed and peeped from behind the curtain when the disciples left his home. With an instinct that Jesus might need protection, Mark had thrown the first garment to hand, a fine linen robe, about his naked body and had crept after the company undetected, waiting while they stopped, creeping into the garden, following Jesus to hide behind a rock as a self-constituted secret guard.

Mark was appalled by the sight and sound of a human being in agony. Jesus prayed, "O my Father, everything is possible with you. Take this cup away from me. Yet, not what I want, but what you want." Again and again came the cry, "Take this cup away." Mark listened and watched, amazed. Jesus was not simply pleading to escape torture, or distress and shame, or physical death in itself. Mark knew from the prophets and psalms that "this cup" meant the wrath of God.

At last Jesus rose from his knees and stumbled toward his three closest friends. John awoke, ashamed to find Jesus standing beside him. Jesus' anguish was now compounded by concern. "Are you asleep?" he said to them. "Could you not watch with me one hour? Stay awake. Pray! Pray, so that you do not fall into temptation." He added, gently, "The spirit is willing but the flesh is weak." John watched Jesus go back toward the stone, then sleep closed his eyes again.

Mark, from his hiding place, saw Jesus kneel down and heard him pray even more earnestly. Though midnight had passed and the night was cold, the body of Jesus poured with sweat; so great was the pressure on his heart that the sweat which fell on the stone was bloody. "Father, if you are willing, take this cup from me," he prayed again. As a follower put it years later, "He offered up prayers and petitions with loud cries and tears to the one who could save him from death." He knew that his Father would not force him; he could refuse, and leave the world as he had found it.

Jesus continued to pray. Mark, his own heart pounding, heard the words, "My Father, if it is not possible for this cup to be taken away except I drink it, may your will be done." Jesus rose from the stone.

A few yards away John awoke a second time to find Jesus standing beside them. They were speechless with shame. Jesus withdrew, and again sleep proved more powerful than loyalty, and they knew nothing of his further agony before his voice awakened them a third time.

Standing up guiltily, John saw by the moonlight that Jesus was weary, his face marked by suffering, yet at peace.

"Still sleeping and resting?" he said. "The hour has come! The Son of man is betrayed to sinners. Get up! Let us go! The traitor is upon us."

Twenty-one
"I HAVE CONDEMNED INNOCENT BLOOD"

With clank of arms, an approaching force drew nearer. Jesus went toward it. All eleven disciples, awakened from sleep, cowered behind him.

John saw soldiers and Temple police carrying flaming torches on poles, despite the nearly full moon, to hunt down their quarry if he fled through the trees; and lamps in earthenware holders in case he hid in caves. They passed the line of olive trees which marked the edge of the garden. Judas Iscariot detached himself from the soldiers. He strode up to Jesus and shouted, "Greetings, Rabbi!" and gave a disciple's customary mark of respect by kissing Jesus on the hand, only not once but effusively.

"Comrade," asked Jesus, "are you betraying the Son of man with a kiss?" Judas did not answer.

"Do what you came for," said Jesus.

Behind Judas emerged an excessively large body of Roman soldiers with swords, Jewish Temple police with cudgels, officials sent by the Sanhedrin, and a gaggle of servants and idlers who had stayed up late on Passover night. But when Jesus stood calmly awaiting arrest without a fight, they were nonplussed.

"Whom do you want?" he asked.

"Jesus of Nazareth!"

"*I am,*" said Jesus. John, though in mounting terror, saw that the words literally made them stagger, for to the Jewish officials in front, with Judas beside them, Jesus had declared himself in that sacred phrase which God alone might use. His majesty of bearing underlined it and caught them off balance, and they fell back, stumbling into the soldiers behind.

Jesus repeated his question as they picked themselves up. Again they answered, "Jesus of Nazareth."

"I told you, *I am!* If you want me, let these men go."

A disciple shouted, "Lord, shall we strike with the swords?" Before Jesus could answer, Peter drew his short sword and struck out wildly, slicing off the right ear of a man whom John recognized as Malthus, a body servant of the high priest.

"Sheathe your sword!" Jesus ordered. Whatever he had meant when encouraging them to bring swords, he rebuked Peter: "Those who take the sword shall perish by the sword. Do you think I cannot call on my Father for more than twelve legions of angels?"—36,000 heavenly beings poised to rescue—"But how would the Scriptures be fulfilled, that it must happen this way? Shall I not drink the cup my Father has given me?"

Jesus stepped up to the shocked, bleeding Malthus who desperately held his ear to his head, and healed him. All the fight went out of Peter.

Jesus turned to the Jewish officials and chief priests. "Am I a brigand, that you come against me with swords and cudgels? Every day I taught in the Temple, and you did not touch me. But this is your hour, the hour of—"

John heard no more. He did not stand his ground when his colleagues' courage collapsed. Peter fled; James fled; Andrew fled; every one of the Twelve ran for their lives, except Judas.

The Roman officer was growing impatient. He gave a sharp command. Soldiers seized Jesus and bound his arms tightly behind his back—brigand or prophet, what did a soldier care?

Someone suddenly saw young Mark. He had come to Gethsemane to protect Jesus, but the display of force and the flight of Peter, whom he had regarded as a rock, drained Mark's valor.

Hands grasped his linen garment. Mark shook himself free and fled naked into the night.

John recovered his nerve quickly. He turned back in time to see the soldiers march Jesus out of the garden and into the ravine. With newfound courage, John edged nearer in the darkness and followed them round the Pool of Siloam and into the lower city. He felt a tug on his sleeve and saw a shaken, irresolute Peter. Together, they went on, keeping behind the marching troops whose torches made shadows dance in the darkened streets. The procession crossed the Tyropoeon Valley and at last reached the high priest's palace on the farther hill, more than a mile from Gethsemane. The gates opened to admit police, servants, prisoner, and traitor, leaving the Roman soldiers to return to barracks.

John, being known to the high-priestly household, had no difficulty in joining the tail of the escort as they jostled into the courtyard. Peter did not dare enter. The gates clanged shut.

John saw Jesus, his arms stiff from the cord, being roughly escorted toward the wing occupied by Annas, the old man who had been high priest until deposed by the Romans fifteen years before; most Jews regarded Annas as equally high priest with his son-in-law Caiaphas, holding that the office was for life. They reckoned the shrewd and patriotic Annas to be still the dominant power.

When John saw where Jesus would be interrogated, he went back and spoke to the girl porter, who opened the gate to admit Peter. She looked at Peter as he crossed the flickering pool of light. Half recognizing him, she said, "You are not one of that man's disciples, are you?"

"I am not," said Peter.

Police and servants, cold from the night march to Gethsemane, had lit a charcoal fire in the courtyard. Peter crept near, trying to warm himself undetected. Behind him the girl stayed at the gate as members of the Sanhedrin, awakened by messages, arrived from their homes and hurried toward the great hall of the palace. John left Peter and quietly joined the priests and scribes watching the preliminary interrogation. He edged himself as close as he could to Jesus, who stood bound before Annas.

Annas was asking questions. Suspects should cringe before him and answer in tones of abject humility; Jesus, however, did not cringe, nor would he name his disciples nor provide information about his teaching. He had said nothing in secret, he replied, but had taught openly in synagogues and in the Temple; and John remembered that even when instructing in private, Jesus urged his disciples to shout from the housetops what he taught. He had nothing to hide. "Why question me?" was all he would say to Annas. "Question the people who heard me. Ask them what I told them. They know what I said."

"How dare you talk disrespectfully to the high priest!" said a guard, and slapped his face.

The welt showed up raw, but Jesus rebuked his assailant: "If I have said anything wrong, tell everyone here what it was. But if I am right in what I have said, why do you hit me?"

Annas suspended his interrogation, for a quorum of Sanhedrin members would have gathered round Caiaphas. Annas ordered the guards to march Jesus to the great hall.

Across the wide courtyard with its huddle of figures round a fire, and up low steps, they led him into the main building of the palace, and placed him under the light of torches flaming in the portico. Peter and those around the fire could see Jesus clearly. In front of him in the great hall sat Caiaphas on his judgment bench, flanked by elders of both Sadducee and Pharisee parties. Judas, the priests and the scribes, with John still unaccosted among them, gathered on one side.

No pleader or advocate rose to make a formal charge. John remembered what Nicodemus had told him, months earlier: Caiaphas was determined to see to it that Jesus would be put to death. But if this was to be done by judicial process, the Roman governor alone had power to impose a death sentence. Caiaphas and his friends needed grounds on which to secure conviction. They had retained witnesses, it seemed, and had summoned them when Judas told where Jesus might be arrested.

The witnesses now testified. They were important, for a bad case would be thrown out by the governor; moreover, John could see that Nicodemus and Joseph of Arimathea, though secret sympathizers, were alert for justice. As the night wore on and the shadows thrown by the moon altered shapes, John heard the witnesses, one after another, fail to substantiate their testimony, or admit to relying on hearsay, or contradict each other. The trial, if it could be called that, offered hope after all, since the governor heard cases at sunrise and time pressed. Jesus might be acquitted through lack of evidence.

Two more witnesses came forward. One deposed: "We heard this fellow say, 'Destroy this Temple made by human hands, and in three days I will build another, not man made.' " But the other witness recalled a different version of words spoken when Jesus first cleared the Temple, three years before. No charge could stick if the evidence was contradictory—unless the prisoner incriminated himself. Jesus had kept silent throughout the proceedings in the great hall.

Caiaphas stood up. "Are you not going to answer? What is this testimony that these men bring against you?"

All eyes turned on Jesus. He stayed silent.

Caiaphas said, "I charge you under oath by the living God: *Are you Messiah, the Son of the Blessed One?*"

"I am!" replied Jesus. He had not merely answered a question. He had again used the sacred phrase which, in the context, had one meaning only. He added, "And you will see the Son of man sitting on the right hand of the Almighty and coming on the clouds of heaven."

At that, the high priest solemnly tore his robe to express formal abhorrence of the mocking of the majesty of God. No further witnesses were needed. "You have heard his blasphemy, what is your verdict?"

They condemned him as worthy of death. Nicodemus and Joseph of Arimathea dissented but were powerless.

The high priest gave a curt order. The guards blindfolded Jesus, then spat at his face, and pummeled him with fists.

Priests, scribes, and retainers ran forward to spit or strike, shouting, "Prophesy! Tell us who hit you," and thereby absolved themselves from being accessories to blasphemy. Flinching at the blows, John recognized that they were also submitting Jesus to a traditional test: according to the scribes' interpretation of the eleventh chapter of Isaiah, the true Messiah would be able to see blindfolded. John's mind clutched at the opportunity which Jesus was given to save himself. Jesus declined to take it; he stayed silent.

Yet at the moment when the Council was deciding that he was not a true prophet, his prophecy to Peter was fulfilled. During the trial of Jesus in the great hall, a lesser trial took place in the courtyard. A slave girl peered at Peter as he warmed himself. "This man was with him," she told the knot of servants and police sitting round the fire.

"Woman, I do not know him!" said Peter. A cock crowed outside the palace, but Peter was oblivious to the meaning. He moved away from the fire toward the gate where the girl porter had half identified him when John had brought him in. This girl repeated to bystanders her earlier belief that he was the prisoner's disciple (and therefore possibly dangerous). When the trial in the great hall was nearing its climax, one of those who had been in Gethsemane, a relative of the servant injured by Peter's sword, accosted him. The man said, "Surely I saw you in the garden. This man is certainly a Galilean—you are one of them!"

"Man, I am not!"

"But your accent gives you away!"

Peter denied with an oath and swore curses on himself if he knew Jesus, while across the courtyard came the shouts and the sounds of blows as they hit the blindfolded Jesus.

The cock crowed a second time. Peter glanced up. In the torchlight he saw the guards remove the blindfold. As the cockcrow died away, Jesus turned and looked straight at Peter. Peter remembered. The gate stood open. He stumbled out into the street weeping bitterly.

John saw him go; and a few minutes later he saw another of the Twelve go into the night, just before dawn. John had watched Judas during the trial. When Judas heard the verdict, his face contorted and he yelled, "I have condemned innocent blood."

An underling of Caiaphas retorted, "What do we care? That is your affair."

Judas threw the thirty pieces of silver on the floor and ran out of the palace.

Twenty-two
"AWAY WITH HIM!"

The Sanhedrin paused briefly until first light before condemning Jesus formally, because a judgment pronounced in the hours of darkness was invalid. Then they had him marched through the dawn the short distance to the palace built by Herod the Great which the prefect of Judea (the Roman governor) used as his praetorium when visiting Jerusalem. Herod had chosen the site of King David's citadel, on high ground adjoining the wall at the northwestern corner of the upper city.

John had no difficulty in following undetected among the priests, scribes, and household servants. At sunrise he was waiting with them, behind the prisoner and some of his judges, in the street of the Upper Market, just outside the wide, open forecourt known as the Pavement. It contained the raised stone *bema*, the tribunal where the governor sat to give verdicts, pronounce sentence, or issue formal orders with force of law. To one side stood the barracks. Ahead, through shady colonnades, were the audience chambers and halls where he heard cases and received deputations and entertained, and behind these a smaller yard led to his private quarters.

Pontius Pilate, the Roman knight from the mountains of southern Italy, who had been prefect of Judea for the past four years, had risen at his usual hour before dawn. At first light he had entered the public rooms to meet heads of departments, hear police reports, and receive petitioners, or transact other business. He knew that the Sanhedrin would bring before him a troublemaker, for he had authorized an armed detachment for the arrest, but no Jews awaited him; it was the Day of Passover, and strict Jews regarded all Gentile houses as ritually unclean. To enter would defile a man for seven days and would ruin his Passover celebrations. Pilate was not surprised therefore when a household slave reported that the Sanhedrin representatives had arrived with their prisoner but refused to enter the palace.

Pilate had learned through much irritation and bloodshed to honor Jews in minor matters. Soon after sunrise he went out to the Pavement, saw the prisoner and his accusers and stood beside the stone *bema* to put the formal question in Greek: "What charge do you bring against this man?"

They did not give a direct answer. Blasphemy was no offense in Roman law unless a man blasphemed the divine emperor, a crime silently committed by every devout Jew, but they hoped Pilate would dispatch Jesus by administrative decision, without trial, as a disturber of the peace. This was within a prefect's prerogative; Pilate had slaughtered Jews readily enough in his first four years. They therefore named no specific crime.

"If he were not a criminal," said the Sanhedrin spokesman, also in Greek, "we would not have brought him before you."

Since the prisoner did not appear to be the usual run of troublemaker, Pilate demanded details. They still hedged. "Take him yourselves, then," said Pilate, "and judge him according to your law."

"We have no right to execute," they replied.

Sometimes they stoned or strangled a man without being called to account, especially if a Gentile trespassed into the inner courts of the Temple; but as John now realized from what Jesus had warned, Caiaphas was determined that Jesus should die by the Roman capital punishment of crucifixion. When a man was crucified, whether on a standing tree near the place of his crime or, more usually, on a tree trunk erected at a crossroads or on a hill, he hung from the tree by nails in his palms or wrists and his feet, until he died a lingering death. Every Jew knew from Scripture that anyone hanged on a tree was cursed. If, therefore, Jesus was crucified he would die under a curse and be exposed as a false messiah. Were he stoned, his disciples might revere him as a martyr; if he hung on a tree they must abhor him or share his curse.

To have him crucified, the Sanhedrin needed to prove that Jesus was guilty of a crime against Rome. The spokesman threw before the governor somewhat incoherent charges of subversion; and that Jesus had urged nonpayment of taxes to Caesar; "and calls himself Christ, a king."

Pilate asked the prisoner to state his defense. Jesus stayed silent. His silence amazed the governor and clearly disturbed him: Roman justice disliked absence of a defense as much as lack of clear charges. Pilate seemed to hesitate, then he withdrew, ordering that Jesus be marched inside. The prosecution refused to defile themselves by entering too; Pilate had guessed correctly. He could question the prisoner without his accusers.

The interview would not be private; John knew that anyone willing to accept defilement could enter the audience chamber, and he at once mounted the steps and walked across the Pavement, mingling with Gentile hangers-on to stay near Jesus and listen. Pilate's questions and Jesus' answers, both in Greek, impressed themselves unforgettably on John's memory.

"Are you the king of the Jews?"

"Is this your own question, or have others told you about me?"

"Am I a Jew?" Pilate spoke in a tone of contempt. "Your own people and the chief priests have brought you before me. What have you done?"

"My kingdom is not of this world. If it were, my servants would be fighting to prevent my arrest by the Jewish leaders. My kingdom is not here."

"Then you are a king?"

"It is you who say that I am a king." In words that opened new vistas of time and eternity if Pilate would look, Jesus went on: "For this I was born—for this I came into the world: to bear witness to the truth. Everyone who is on the side of truth listens to me."

"What is truth?" said Pilate. He did not wait for an answer, and the world has teased ever since over his meaning: whether he jested, or feared to pursue the subject, or had satisfied himself that Jesus was not guilty. A Roman magistrate was trained to seek out truth, but Jesus had placed a disturbing meaning on the word.

Pilate left him in the audience chamber and went out to the Pavement. "I find no case for this man to answer," he announced.

The Sanhedrin spokesman refused to accept the verdict. Their shouts reverberated across the Pavement as they cried out that Jesus had caused disaffection by his teaching throughout Judea: he had started in Galilee and now was here.

At the name "Galilee," Pilate pricked up his ears. If Jesus were a Galilean subject, he could be sent across to Herod Archelaus, the Tetrarch. Although an arrested man need not be returned to his own jurisdiction, as formerly, this could be done if a governor preferred. Pilate told the prosecution to lay the case before Herod. The accusers marched Jesus out of the audience chamber. John slipped out too, hoping that Jesus had caught sight of him and knew that one friend was near.

While they were on the way to Herod, Pilate went on with the next cases. The first two ended swiftly: two thieves were proved guilty of sedition. Pilate ascended the *bema* and pronounced sentence: "I consign you to the cross." Each robber was immediately removed to the barracks to suffer the first stage of the punishment—a violent flogging. Provincials were always executed on the day of sentence. No appeal lay open except for Roman citizens, of any race, who might appeal to Caesar. Nor might Roman citizens be executed by crucifixion: it was regarded as so cruel, slow, and disgusting a death that it could be used only for slaves and low provincials.

Pilate started hearing the third case. This soon developed complications. The brigand Barabbas, who had committed murder in a recent rebellion, was a popular freedom fighter or Zealot, and his friends had swarmed up from the stews of the lower city to watch his trial. They began to shout that Pilate should follow custom and mark the Passover by releasing one prisoner chosen by popular acclamation. They wanted Barabbas. Friends of Jesus also swelled the crowd; news of his arrest was all over the city. Some who had heard him in the Temple, along with fellow pilgrims from Galilee, had come to the Pavement and would shout for Jesus. The crowd grew every minute; the mass of Jews from every land, packing Jerusalem for the festival, included many who were avid for excitement.

Meanwhile, Jesus had been arraigned before Herod the Tetrarch. Sitting on a throne in his lesser palace, the superstitious Herod, who had admired John the Baptist yet killed him, showed pleasure at the opportunity to satisfy his curiosity about Jesus and perhaps to see a miracle. The prosecution hurled charges. Jesus declined to utter one word of rebuttal. Herod questioned Jesus, but he did not answer. Herod soon tired of the case, but whereas Pilate was perplexed, Herod took Jesus as a joke. The Tetrarch and his army captains turned Jesus into a king of the revels. They arrayed him in a gorgeous robe, made fun of him, and returned him, still silent, to Pilate.

As all stood again at the Pavement, it became obvious to John that Pilate more than ever wanted to release Jesus, whom neither he nor Herod had found guilty of a capital crime. Moreover, a messenger came from the private quarters and told Pilate that his wife, disturbed by a dream, urged him to have nothing to do with "that innocent man." But Pilate the judge was also Pilate the politician who did not wish to anger the Jewish leaders; they could make life wearisome or complain to Caesar. He decided to shift responsibility from his shoulders by acceding to the demand for the festival amnesty by popular acclaim. Conviction or acquittal by the people was not unusual in the Roman Empire, and he trusted that the vote would go to the right man; otherwise, Barabbas would resume his career of insurrection, murder, pillage of caravans, and nocturnal harassment of soldiers.

Neither prisoner had yet been formally condemned. Pilate mounted the stone *bema* and proposed to the crowd that he should have Jesus beaten, to teach him a lesson, and then released. The lictors would beat him with rods—the lesser form of corporal punishment, such as Paul and Silas suffered at Philippi. It was frequently ordered as a warning, or when a man was a nuisance to the authorities, and generally was administered in public to shame a man before his neighbors.

Pilate put the question. "Shall I release to you the king of the Jews?" They would first have to watch their king being beaten; the whole episode of kingship would fizzle out in absurdity.

Shouts came back from the crowd: "Not this man but Barabbas." Shouts for Jesus were drowned as the priests stirred up the people for Barabbas. The priests turned any confusion to Barabbas' advantage until the calls for his release grew overwhelming.

"What shall I do with Jesus who is called Christ?" asked Pilate.

"Crucify him! Let him be crucified," roared the crowd.

Pilate hesitated again. The sole responsibility for life or for death was his. He sensed that to settle the case of Jesus by acclamation would now be a miscarriage of justice, yet he shied from an acquittal in the face of near riot. His contemporary, the Jewish philosopher Philo of Alexandria, described Pilate as "by nature rigid and stubbornly harsh"; yet when confronted with Jesus, he wavered.

Pilate saw another way out. As a first step, he ordered Jesus a scourging; to be beaten, not with rods but with the dreaded *flagellum,* which was the preliminary to crucifixion, yet could be treated as a sentence in itself or as part of the interrogation of a suspect. When the crowd saw what was left of him, Pilate reasoned, their sympathy should ensure acquittal.

Syrian soldiers briskly marched Jesus into the barracks. For interrogation, the victim was stretched with hands over his head while a clerk stood by to take down confessions or evidence between screams. But they led Jesus to a courtyard where a half-pillar, waist high, stood between runnels for washing away the blood: the pillar had been used twice that day for two thieves.

John saw it all, as he crept in among those who came and went in the palace. Near to tears, he watched the soldiers strip Jesus naked and bend him over the pillar, tying him so that back, buttocks, and legs were equally exposed. Two burly slaves stood ready, also naked. Each picked up a whip of three leather thongs on which had been strung lumps of bone, and standing on either side of him, they brought down the whips in turn with all their might, to cut through skin, nerves, and muscle. They lashed his shoulders and spinal cord, his buttocks and his thighs. Thongs curled round and cut his chest and ribs. A flogging with the *flagellum* could kill in itself if prolonged, or cripple for life; but a man to be crucified must be left the strength to carry the crossbeam to the site of his execution. The pain was atrocious. When, in after years, followers of Jesus were whipped for their faith, and were conscious of him at their side, they were comforted because he himself knew what they suffered.

Jesus did not cry out. With superhuman strength, he endured the pain in silence. This courage did not move the soldiers. When the flogging stopped and they unbound him and he stood in his blood, shivering from shock, cut and bruised from shoulders to calves, they mocked him. They found a military cloak, near enough in color to the imperial purple, for his nakedness. To John's horror, they fashioned a garland of thorns with spikes which aped a raylike crown of royalty, and thrust it down on his head, so that blood trickled from the temples. They put a rod in his right hand, then knelt before him and crowed, "Hail, king of the Jews."

All their hatred of Jews erupted as they seized the rod and hit him on the head, driving the thorns deeper into his skin. One by one soldiers came up to kneel, to rise and spit on his face, to slap him, infuriated by his silence, his refusal to revile back.

The horseplay stopped when the command came to return Jesus to the Pavement. During the flogging, Pilate had retired within. Now he emerged and the waiting crowd fell quiet. John, choking back his nausea and grief, hurried back too before he could be caught and locked away. He stood in the street and watched Pilate come forward to the edge of the Pavement to address the populace.

"Pay attention," said Pilate. "I am bringing him out to you, to let you know that I find no crime in him."

In total silence all looked toward the barracks. Out of the shadows, slowly and painfully, prodded by soldiers, came Jesus wearing the purple robe and the crown of thorns, his face defiled by spittle and marked by agony, the robe soaked in blood.

"Behold the man!" cried Pilate.

John's heart stood still. On the next moments hung almost the last hope that Jesus would be released and restored to his friends. Then he heard a voice from the crowd call out in a tone of venom, "Crucify!" The cry was taken up, "Crucify! Crucify!"

Pilate had miscalculated his hope of sympathy for the victim. He shouted back, but the tumult grew. John heard priests chant, "We have a law. And by that law he ought to die. Because he claimed to be the Son of God."

Pilate looked nonplussed and scared. He took Jesus inside again. This time the interview was private. John must have heard the details afterward, in happier times, from Jesus himself, and could visualize the scene.

The scarred prisoner, whose majesty seemed more potent than the blood and filth on his person, stood before the governor. "Where do you come from?" asked Pilate.

Jesus said nothing.

"Will you not speak to me? Do you not understand that I have authority to release you or to—*crucify* you?"

Jesus replied through his pain and swollen lips: "You could have no power over me unless it had been granted you from above. Therefore the one who handed me over to you has the greater sin."

Pilate came out on to the Pavement again, alone. John knew that one word from the governor would free Jesus. But the accusers roared, "If you release this man, you are not Caesar's friend! Anyone who claims to be a king opposes Caesar."

Pilate was trapped. If he did his duty and released Jesus, whom he had found innocent, his career might be ruined.

He ordered Jesus to be brought out again.

"Here is your king!"

"Away with him! Crucify!"

"Why, what evil has he done?"

"Crucify! Crucify!"

"Shall I crucify your king?"

"We have no king but Caesar!"

In a calmer moment, Pilate would have relished the irony of the most insolent of subject races proclaiming loyalty. All he could see now was the danger of riot.

He took his seat on the stone *bema* to give sentence for

treason. First, he ordered a bowl of water to be brought. The crowd quieted as they watched him solemnly wash his hands.

"I am not responsible for the death of this innocent man," he said, "It is your doing."

"His blood be on us." their spokesman shouted. "On us and on our children."

Pilate, as guilty of judicial murder as the Jewish leaders, released Barabbas and sentenced Jesus to the cross.

Twenty-three
THE LONELY HILL

Once again there was a pause. In the barracks, the soldiers prepared to crucify the three who had been sentenced. Outside, John waited, determined to be near Jesus to the last. Priests and scribes waited also to see their victim suffer, but the friends of Barabbas had carried him off to celebrate. A company of devout women of Jerusalem, whose custom was to weep and wail for those about to die and to ease their sufferings, came to the edge of the Pavement, ready for service.

On this Friday, April 7, A.D. 30 (the date in modern style which best fits the evidence), the sun was already strong when John heard a sharp command from inside the barracks. A moment later, a young, smart centurion emerged and stood on the steps of the Pavement to supervise the execution squad under his command. First came slaves carrying ladders, ropes, iron nails and hammers; the logs, about six feet long, lay ready for use as crossbeams. Rome ordained that every condemned man carry his own, and soon the two robbers with their flagellated backs lurched into the street under theirs. Each was prodded or beaten forward as necessary by the four soldiers assigned to crucify and afterward guard him.

John saw Jesus come into the sunlight with his four executioners. He wore his own clothes but no one had removed the crown of thorns. Across his shoulders lay a heavy beam which chafed the welts of the flogging and weighed down his body, weak from loss of blood and lack of sleep and food. After a few yards along the street, he staggered, then fell, the log pinning him to the ground. The centurion came up, fearful lest the prisoner die before he could be crucified. Then a soldier caught sight of a strong-looking fellow walking up the street, an African named Simon from Cyrene, who was coming into the city from the country. The centurion exercised his right to order any citizen to carry a load one mile and commanded him to take the crossbeam. Since later Simon's two sons, Alexander and Rufus, became members of the Christian community, the experience must have changed his life.

Relieved of his burden, Jesus walked steadily between his executioners. The devout women began their wailing and weeping, but Jesus turned and begged them not to weep for him. He warned them to weep rather for themselves and their children because of the miseries that would fall on Jerusalem.

Behind the women followed a small crowd: the priests who would witness the execution on behalf of the Sanhedrin; a medley of ghoulish spectators; and his friends and the sympathizers of those about to die. John had been joined by Jesus' mother. Mary was bravely determined to stay by her son in his last hours, however terrible the sight, and her sister Salome, John's mother, was at her side, with Mary Magdalene and women from Galilee. Peter in his shame was nowhere to be seen, but by his own statement long afterward he was "a witness of the sufferings of Christ"—unnoticed, far off, alone with his thoughts and tears. If any others of the Twelve had begun to recover their souls, they find no place in the record. Judas was dead by his own hand.

The procession moved through the street toward the gate. Dogs ran between legs or scurried off yelping when a soldier kicked. John saw Jews about their daily business, and pilgrims sightseeing, who traditionally hurried out of the way of an execution squad, many turning faces to the wall to avoid so unpleasant a sight. But John saw Jews who wept when they recognized Jesus and joined in behind to support him.

Passing through the Garden Gate of the city, the executioners and those who followed moved a little way beyond the walls to where the ground began to rise to the western hill overlooking Jerusalem. They stopped on a rocky outcrop with contours which fitted its name, Place of the Skull (*Golgotha* in Aramaic, *Calvarius* in Latin). It was dominated by tree trunks erected for crucifixions, used again and again as men were taken down dead. Disused quarries close by made quick burials convenient, in the old workings. Calvary's one pleasant feature was the nearness of the gardens beyond, including one which belonged to Joseph of Arimathea.

The centurion made a brief inspection of the site and spoke to his sergeant, who barked an order at the two robbers. They dropped their beams, each before a tree trunk to left and right. The sergeant told Simon of Cyrene to lay his beam beside the tree in the center. The centurion had in his charge a placard about Jesus and wanted him, as the only prominent convict, to die between the others.

The slaves leaned ladders against the uprights and arranged ropes. The devout women now carried out their permitted charity. They handed to the executioners, to pass to their victims, the drugged wine which would deaden some of the pain. Beheading was comparatively painless and swift; crucifixion was slow and literally excruciating. John saw the two thieves gratefully swallow every drop of the drugged wine, but when a soldier brought a wineskin to Jesus, he tasted the mixture, shook his head, and handed it back with unfailing courtesy. John then took Mary, Salome, and the women to a spot where they would not be able to see or hear too closely what was about to happen. He left them there and returned. Determined to comfort Jesus, standing as near as the soldiers allowed, he steeled himself to watch.

While the other squads worked on the thieves, the four executioners laid their hands on Jesus and stripped him naked, even tearing away the loincloth portrayed in Christian art: the Romans did not vary their practice because circumcised Jews abhorred nudity, since shame, and affront to human dignity, were part of the punishment. A man was crucified naked whether Gentile or Jew.

Then they threw Jesus to the ground: they never took chances with a criminal, who might make a last desperate struggle to avoid his fate. John longed to plead with them to be gentle, knowing that Jesus would not resist, but the plea would fall on deaf ears; the men cared nothing that his back was torn and tender, or that his head was circled by thorns. Two soldiers stretched out his arms, a third pushed the crossbeam under them while the fourth pressed hard against his knees.

A soldier picked up a long iron nail and a hammer, knelt on one of Jesus' arms and poised the nail above the palm.

With a sharp blow on the nail, he drove it through his hand into the crossbeam. John clapped his hands to his ears, but suddenly realized that the involuntary reaction of Jesus' vocal chords to the shock and pain was not a scream but the cry "*Abba,* Father." Each blow increased the pain, and the second soldier had started on the palm of the other hand. From behind him, John could hear the thieves being nailed down, to screams and curses and obscenities, but Jesus did not scream; he prayed. In gasps and gulps, the words came clear between the hammer blows: "Father, forgive them. They know not what they do."

John marveled, and his mounting hatred of his Master's executioners began to turn, in spite of himself, to love. And the prayer would be answered; John recalled Jesus' words to the Father, "I know that you hear me always." The soldiers now callously piercing and soon to mock Jesus would one day seek him to accept the forgiveness, perhaps far away in another land (indeed, one may have provided the vivid close-up memories used by Luke in his Gospel).

At present, the executioners seemed unaware that their cruelty under orders had met with love instead of hate. They drove the nails home and wiped the blood from their hands.

One of them climbed the ladder. Others lifted the beam with Jesus nailed to it, and thus caused the most dreadful pain as jolt by jolt they hoisted him by ropes and secured the beam with cords to the upright so that his body's weight pressed down on a stout horn or peg projecting between the crotch. They crossed his legs, forced the feet against the tree, and drove a nail through each. Their experience of crucifying ensured that every nail went where it would stay in place.

The soldiers removed ladder and ropes and left Jesus to hang by the nails, his feet a little way off the ground. One soldier stood guard, and when John wanted to brush away the flies and stinging insects, he was ordered roughly away, and forced to watch impotently as the torture wracked his best friend. The blood which flowed from the nail wounds in hands and feet began to congeal, but whenever Jesus struggled for breath it would start again. John could only guess at the agony: the cramps shooting through inert arms and legs, the suppurating of wounds from the flogging and the thorns and the nails; the pitiless sun and the thirst, already raging from shock.

A soldier put up the ladder again and hammered to the wood above Jesus' head the placard handed him by the centurion to proclaim the name and crimes of the crucified in Aramaic, Latin, and Greek: *Jesus of Nazareth, the king of the Jews*. The Sanhedrin's witnesses at once objected, "He *claimed* to be king of the Jews." The centurion shrugged his shoulders and told them that any complaint should be made to the governor. Two chief priests hurried off to demand audience. When they returned after not too long an interval, they were angry. They told the others that Pilate had snubbed them. "What I have written, I have written," he had said, a snub even more terse since he spoke in Greek: "*Ho gegrapha, gegrapha*."

In their anger they threw pity to the winds and hurled insults at Jesus as he hung immobile on the cross . "He saved others but he can't save himself," they jeered. "He is the king of Israel! Let him come down from the cross, and we will believe in him. He trusts in God. Let God rescue him now if He wants him, for he said, 'I am the Son of God.' " Crowds who had poured out of the city and travelers on the highway took up the cry, and threw his own words back at him and taunted him. The soldiers who had sat down to share out his clothes as their perk, and toss for the seamless robe, mocked him with his title, sneering, "If you are the

king of the Jews, save yourself!" The crucified thieves joined
in the insults, as if to relieve their own agony and fury before
their voices should lapse into croaks.

One of the two thieves, suffering the same physical torture
as Jesus, must have observed, as John had, Jesus' patience as
fresh pains shot through his nailed body, his refusal to revile
those who reviled him, his quiet dignity in disgrace, even a
touch of joy as if he could see beyond the lingering death to
somewhere wonderful. This thief fell silent, but his fellow,
after writhing again in an attempt to relieve the pressure on
his pinioned hands, taunted Jesus, "If you are the Christ,
save yourself and us!" His voice was now scarcely audible
beyond the crosses, but the other heard and rebuked him.
"We are getting what we deserved for our crimes. This man
has done nothing wrong." Painfully he turned his head to
the cross between them. "Jesus," he said, "remember me
when you come into your kingdom."

Jesus mustered strength to turn his head. "Truly I tell
you," he replied, "today you will be with me in paradise."

John's attention had been fixed on Jesus and only now did
he become aware that Mary, leaning on his own mother
Salome, had moved in from the spot where distance had
blurred the harrowing sight of her son being nailed down
and mounted on the cross. John supported her, and together
they looked up at Jesus and saw in his face his love for Mary
and gratitude for her courage and devotion, and John's.
Tenderly, he gave each into the care of the other.

John held Mary close, and henceforth his home would be
Mary's. But Mary would not leave the cross; they stood
there, unable to grasp a thought except that Jesus hung in
dreadful pain and would die. Grief, perplexity, and defeat
had driven from their minds his words about why he must
die and his promise that he would see them again. A little

way off, not obtruding, stood Salome and Mary Magdalene and a few other close friends. Behind them, farther away and beyond those who reviled Jesus, were bystanders who sorrowed. They had sat at his feet and admired his words and deeds yet now had lost all hope; he hung dying on a cross, and their belief was dying with him, that he would redeem their land and people.

By now, after nearly three hours, the torture had worked its havoc on Jesus' body until he was an even more horrifying sight. The physical beauty which matched his goodness had gone; he was contorted, disfigured, despicable. Blood dripped from his hands and feet. Lips and face and limbs were blotched by sun blisters and insect bites. The stripes where the scourge had curled round his chest and stomach and legs showed vivid against his skin. His bones stuck out from the flesh.

At noon a new horror began. Darkness covered the land: not an eclipse of the sun, for this was the day of full moon. The strange loss of light which precedes an earthquake would have had a small part in it, but whatever its extent and physical cause, the untimely darkness quieted mockers, and increased the anguish of Mary and John, for Jesus seemed enveloped by evil. His face showed signs of a struggle more fearful than the pain from wounds or mockery—as if he were indeed under a curse while hanging on a tree, and looking into the abyss with a horror of a great darkness invading his soul, and loathsome all about him. An invisible weight bore down upon his shoulders. As time passed, infinitely slowly without movement of shadows, Mary and John clung desperately to each other, unable to help him. This was no joyous martyr's death: Jesus sank into sorrow to a depth beyond imagination. His grief was fearful to behold.

After three hours of darkness, Jesus gave a sudden terrible

cry, startling in its strength and clarity: *"Eloi, eloi, lama sabachthani?"* Mary and John were appalled. He had cried, "My God, my God. Why have you forsaken me?" He had spoken the opening words of *Psalm 22*, but the force of his cry left them in no doubt that the question had been wrung with full meaning from the bottom of his being.

Soldiers and others who were not familiar with Aramaic shouted, "He is calling for Elijah!" A little later Jesus spoke again. "I thirst." A soldier soaked a sponge into their ration of wine vinegar, wedged it on a hyssop stick, and put it up to Jesus' lips and he drank. Other bystanders were callous: "Leave him alone. Let's see whether Elijah will come and take him down."

A few more minutes passed. The breath came in short gasps as if he were dying already, though a man crucified in the prime of life might take three days to die. John could hardly bear to look and was too broken to recall Jesus' words in his great sermon on the Good Shepherd: "No man takes my life from me; I lay it down myself. I have authority to lay it down and to take it again."

Suddenly Jesus gave another cry, its tone not of desertion but of triumph: "It is finished!" A moment later John heard him say, "Father, into your hands I commit my spirit." Gently, Jesus bowed his head with its crown of thorns. A second later his body hung utterly still.

The ground shook in an earth tremor, strong enough to split rocks in the nearby quarries, while in the Temple, half a mile off, the great curtain which blocked the way into the Holy of Holies tore in half from top to bottom.

As the earthquake ceased, the darkness lifted. The executioners stood white and awestruck. The Roman centurion looked up at the corpse of Jesus and said, "Surely that man was the Son of God."

Part Three
GLORIOUS
MORNING

Twenty-four
THE EMPTY
TOMB

The body of Jesus hung stiff in the afternoon light. John would not have been allowed to remove it for burial because exposure, alive and dead, was part of the sentence of crucifixion. Very occasionally, guards left an execution too soon and a crucified man was removed by his friends, who might try to revive him, but the two and a half hours during which Jesus hung dead on the cross removed all hope. John could do nothing but keep off the scavenger birds.

Mary still refused to leave. The other women, engulfed by sorrow, withdrew a little way off, uncertain what to do. Priests and scribes walked away toward the city, many looking shaken; some even beat their chests in a gesture of repentance. To the left and right of Jesus' body, the two thieves feebly struggled for breath. The torture, exposure, and starvation had reduced them to little more than conscious corpses, yet a whole night might pass before they died.

An official messenger came up to the centurion. Pilate wanted to know if it were true that Jesus had died so early in his crucifixion. The centurion sent the messenger back with confirmation.

The corpse on the cross stiffened with rigor mortis. The thieves moaned feebly and struggled to force air into their lungs by lifting their chests.

About an hour before sunset, John saw a picket of soldiers. They carried spears and iron mallets, and when they reported to the centurion, John overheard that Pilate had agreed to a request from Caiaphas: no dying or dead bodies should pollute the high Sabbath of Passover by hanging outside the city wall. A soldier walked up to each thief, lifted a mallet, and with brutal efficiency smashed his knees and legs. Weak cries gave little indication of the searing pain, but death rattles followed soon, for when a crucified man could no longer put pressure on his legs, he lost the last power to lift his ribs and breathe.

The soldiers converged on Jesus. He looked dead; to make death certain, a soldier jabbed him in the side with a spear, causing a wound large enough for a hand to be inserted. John saw a sudden gush of blood and water. A plausible medical explanation is that an internal hemorrhage, caused by the flogging, had settled in the rib cage.

Hardly had the soldiers completed their work when Joseph of Arimathea and Nicodemus, with servants carrying bundles of linen and bags of spices, approached the central cross. The two Sanhedrin counselors had thrown off the secrecy of their allegiance to Jesus and had boldly asked Pilate for permission to remove and bury the body. On receiving the centurion's report, Pilate granted their request since they were men of rank in good standing; permission was seldom refused except in cases of high treason on the part of the criminal.

As the evening shadows lengthened, John watched, numbed with sorrow, the gruesome work of extracting the nails with iron pincers, lowering the rigid arms, and laying the corpse of Jesus on the ground. Then Mary swooned at last, and when the women had revived her, John took her away, walking in their grief through the city to the home of John Mark.

It was not until dusk, therefore, a few moments before Sabbath began, and Mary Magdalene and the other women reached the house, that John Mark heard what happened.

Nicodemus had brought spices in great weight, as for a king's burial. Joseph had brought unbleached linen to make a shroud and a napkin for the head. Jews did not gut a corpse as the Egyptians did, and the two eminent counselors and their servants, in their hurry to complete the burial before Sabbath, wrapped the body of Jesus unwashed, but with reverence. They carried it the short distance to Joseph of Arimathea's garden. Joseph had planned to be buried there himself and had hewn out a new tomb from the hillside which sheltered his vegetables and shrubs. Since Jesus had no family tomb in Jerusalem, nor was there time to look farther, they laid him in this rich man's grave.

Mary Magdalene and her companions, following at a distance, saw the burial party stoop to enter the tomb. Inside, a shelf had been hewn from the rock. The two counselors emerged; their men, sweating and straining, heaved into position the great boulder which blocked the entrance. The women saw it all, then hurried back to the city.

John, Mary, and the other women spent the night and day of Sabbath in mute despair. Their world had collapsed. Neither the ancient prophets nor the recent words of Jesus could penetrate their grief. Bereft of him, they had lost hope and purpose. No one had heart to attend synagogue or Temple, but friends who called to offer sympathy spoke of a city divided. Many held high festival while others were perplexed by the sudden condemnation and horrifying death of Jesus. No one, however, told them that Caiaphas had sent chief priests into Pilate's palace on a high Sabbath, thereby ritually defiling themselves, to warn him that the disciples might steal the body and then announce that Jesus had risen from the dead; "this last deception will be worse than the first." Pilate wearily allowed the priests' request to mount their own guard and to put a seal on the tomb, a task which broke the Sabbath.

Had the women known about the guards they might not have had courage to do what they did next morning: they knew only about the huge stone, and were worried how they should move it.

As soon as Sabbath ended at sunset on the Saturday, Mary Magdalene, Salome, and another Mary (whose two sons were also among the eleven disciples) hurried to the re-opened shops and bought spices. Even if they knew how deeply Nicodemus had embalmed the body, they wanted to add their own fragrance to help offset the stench of decay and to honor Jesus' memory. They mixed the preparation during the night, the second since his death, then tried to sleep.

At dawn on the third day, Sunday, April 9, A.D. 30, while Jesus' mother slept in her grief, the other women crept out at dawn. John watched them go, and could imagine them as they walked as mourners through the wakening streets and through the city gate, which opened at dawn; averting their gaze as they passed the bloodstained crosses, and entering Joseph's garden.

John heard a knock at the door. The maid Rhoda let in Simon Peter. No one knew where he had lodged, though his wife was presumably among the pilgrims. The two men sat together in grief too deep for words while the sun rose and light flooded into the upper room. Soon came other knocks. One by one the Eleven, who could move freely now that Sabbath was over, with other close friends, converged on the house of happy memories to draw strength from each other's sorrow. None recalled past desertions: they were united in grief, wanting only to comfort Mary, his mother.

Suddenly there was a commotion below, and voices and a pounding on the stairs. Mary Magdalene, Salome, and the other Mary burst into the room.

"They have taken the Lord out of the tomb," cried Mary Magdalene, "and we do not know where they have laid him!"

The women's account was so incoherent and amazing that the first instinct of John, Peter, and the others was to dismiss it as nonsense. No statement of a woman was highly regarded (it had no force in law) and no one noted too precisely what they said, nor unraveled seeming discrepancies afterward, so that their testimony went down into history unpolished and spontaneous.

They had entered the garden, they said, just after sunrise. They saw at once that the stone was no longer at the mouth of the tomb. Armed guards lay on the ground either asleep or dead: the women had not expected to see guards, but they expected to see the body of Jesus when they looked into the tomb. It was gone. While they tried to collect their wits, they saw a vision of angels, dazzling like lightning; but whether two angels or one, whether in the tomb or sitting on the stone, the women could not recall with clarity. They received a message that they were not to be afraid: Jesus was not there, he was risen; he would go to Galilee where they would see him; they must tell his disciples, "and Peter," at once.

They had left the tomb in confusion, shock, and terror and run back to the city, not saying a word to any they passed, and had come at once to the house.

A huge stone had been moved; guards like dead men; dazzling angels; empty tomb—it all sounded idiots' tales. But something had happened.

Peter and John put on their sandals and ran, as if for their lives.

John was fleeter of foot than the more rugged Peter, and once they were free of the workaday streets and through the gate, he outpaced Peter and reached the garden first. The guards were nowhere to be seen. John ran to the tomb. He stooped and looked in and as his eyes grew used to the dark interior he saw no sign of grave robbers. The linen shroud lay all of a piece, not in a heap like Lazarus' graveclothes after Jesus had commanded "loose him," but as if the body had passed through it. He saw the head napkin nearby, which had been around the skull and jaw. It lay folded.

Peter ran up and went straight into the tomb. Then John entered. Without doubt, the tomb and the shroud were empty. John believed the unbelievable: he had not expected what he saw. He did not bring to mind any of the prophecies which Jesus had taught them from Scripture that the Christ would rise from the dead; but he believed.

Peter went out of the tomb very silent. John followed him. Together, they walked away from the garden, followed by two of the women. Mary Magdalene stayed behind, and they heard her beginning to wail again. As they entered the city gate, Peter said not a word. Nor would he return to Mark's home but went off to his lodging.

An hour or two later, while John was trying to focus his thoughts, and the others puzzled over the meaning of the empty tomb, Mary Magdalene came into the house again and ran up the stairs. Her face was radiant: "I have seen the Lord!"

They crowded round her. Her story was one more amazement on that amazing morning. She told how she had stopped her wailing to take another look into the tomb. Where Jesus' body had rested, she saw through her tears a dazzling vision, one angel at the head and the other at the foot.

"Why are you crying?" they asked.

"They have taken away my Lord, and I don't know where they have put him!"

Something made her turn around. Blurred by tears, she saw a Man: no angelic vision this time but a Man so normal and strong, in his early thirties, that she assumed he was the gardener.

She begged this Man to tell her where he had put him, "and I will carry him away."

"Mary!" said the Man.

She could not mistake the voice. She cried, "My own Teacher!" and fell at his feet. Jesus gently told her not to hold him, for he was not yet returned to the Father.

And now Mary Magdalene was bringing the disciples his message. He had called them his brothers and she reported that he had said, "I am returning to my Father and your Father, to my God and your God."

It was only a woman's word. Could she have received a vision? John yearned to see him with his own eyes and to touch him, if only for the second or two which Mary had been allowed, before Jesus returned to the Father.

Mary Magdalene's joy was not infectious; some of them

did not believe her, including Thomas, who had to leave shortly afterward for affairs which would occupy him the remainder of the day, and two who left to journey to Emmaus, seven miles from Jerusalem, in the afternoon. They walked away sad and perplexed.

They had not been gone more than an hour when the door of the house opened and closed again and John heard a heavy step, which could be none other than Peter's, upon the stair. Simon Peter entered the room, and John saw at once that something very wonderful had happened to him. He was subdued yet happy; tears of joy welled in his eyes. All he would say was, "He has appeared to me." He never revealed a word of what passed between them. John, yearning more than ever to see him, recognized the true stamp of Jesus; he had appeared first of all among the Eleven, to the one who loved him yet had denied him.

Though Peter would not disclose private words, most of those present doubted no longer. Whatever the world might say, Jesus had risen from the dead.

During the later afternoon, they learned that Caiaphas and his officials had countered the rumors sweeping the city by circulating statements that while the guards slept, Jesus' disciples had stolen the body. The high priest's next steps might be to discover, arrest, and destroy the disciples so that they could not expose his deceit. They hurriedly bolted the outer and inner doors of Mark's home.

They talked much among themselves. The tomb was empty; Mary had seen him, and he had appeared to Peter and forgiven him; yet they did not know what to do next because the events of the day were beyond human experience. When at dusk Rhoda brought up a meal of broiled fish, honeycomb, and bread, they thankfully sat up at the table and ate. Joy was uppermost in their mood, but grief and surprise were close below.

They were interrupted by a knocking so loud that some feared that the Temple police had discovered them. They heard the doors being unbolted, and excited friendly voices. While the doors were locked again, the two who had gone to Emmaus came running upstairs and into the room. John guessed at once, but before he could speak someone called out to them. "It is true. The Lord has risen! He has appeared to Simon!"

In reply, the two travelers could not contain their own excitement. They had been walking along the highway, they said, trying to understand the events of the past days but unable to throw off their grief, despite the women's story, when a stranger overtook them and joined their conversation. He asked the cause of their sorrow. With their downcast eyes, they did not look searchingly at the face under the headdress, and when he seemed ignorant they told him about the death of the Prophet on whom all their hopes had rested; and of the women's discovery of the empty tomb; and of the dash by Peter and John, who "found it just as the women had said, but they did not see *him*."

The Stranger rebuked them. He called them fools and too slow to believe all that the prophets had spoken about the Christ.

Then he took them through the Scriptures, explaining passages in such a way that their hearts were strangely warmed until on fire. They reached Emmaus. The Stranger apparently was going farther, but with dusk falling they prevailed on him to stay at their house.

They prepared a meal, and it was then, when he took up the bread, gave thanks, broke it, and gave pieces to them from scarred hands, that they realized who he was.

Seconds later he disappeared: the Man whom they had

taken as another foot traveler until the glorious moment of recognition had simply disappeared. They had returned at once to Jerusalem through the dusk and nightfall to bring their news. A stony road and the risk of robbers meant nothing to tired feet impelled by joy.

John had listened with the rest in silence. No shreds of doubt remained, but he yearned even more to see Jesus. Four friends at the least had seen him, yet not John.

They were all talking excitedly when they heard the unmistakable voice of Jesus: "*Shalom*. Peace be with you." They looked and he was there, standing at the table among them, even though the doors were locked. They had longed for him; but, taken by surprise, they were terrified, wondering if they were seeing his ghost. The shattered corpse of Calvary was alive, in normal health, wearing his usual clothes, with that smile they would never forget. Despite hopes and belief that he had risen, his unexpected coming threw them in turmoil.

He spoke again. "Why are you troubled? Why do doubts rise in your minds? Look at my hands and my feet. It is I, myself! Touch me and see. A ghost does not have flesh and bones as you see that I have!"

He held out his hands, and the holes made by the nails were plain to their eyes. He made them look at his feet; they saw where the nails had pierced. When they were still speechless with joy and amazement, and some seemed still to doubt, he asked for something to eat. They gave him some fish and honeycomb, and he ate.

He sat down. As they relaxed he looked around and taught them just as in old times.

He recalled how he had told them that the prophecies about Christ would be fulfilled in him, and he began to take them through the Scriptures, as he had taken the two on the

Emmaus road, showing that Christ had to suffer for the sins of mankind and then rise from the dead and enter his glory. Scripture after Scripture had been fulfilled in detail, by men acting unawares, such as the soldiers who had not broken his legs but had pierced him, and the counselors who had buried him in a rich man's grave.

By now all those present were overjoyed. Jesus said again, "*Shalom.* Peace be with you," and told them that they would continue his work of bringing men the forgiveness of sins.

He did not stay with them. Nor did he reappear the next day. Thomas, indeed, when he returned to their company, even refused to believe that they had seen him.

Thomas told them that unless he could see the nail marks himself, "and put my finger where the nails were, and put my hand into his side, I will *not* believe." Nothing they could say changed his mind, and still Jesus did not meet any of them, nor confront his persecutors. Days passed; doubt gnawed a little.

On the following Sunday evening, they were again gathered, including Thomas, in the Upper Room, as if instinctively celebrating the Resurrection one week later. Expectancy rose high and was not disappointed. The doors were locked, yet Jesus joined them and their hearts leaped to hear his "*Shalom!*"

He beckoned immediately to Thomas.

"Put your finger here and see my hands," He said. "Reach out your hand and put it in my side. Stop doubting, and believe."

Thomas did not lift his finger, but answered, "My Lord and my God!"

Twenty-five
WITH YOU ALWAYS

One afternoon later that April the Sea of Galilee sparkled in the spring sunshine which touched scores of sails. Across the deep blue of the water, the eastern shore showed clear, with the wooded hills behind. Mount Hermon's snow hung hazily above the horizon to the north. The scene looked familiar; time might have stood still since the spring day three years before when John had jumped onto the beach from his father's ship to meet Jesus.

This afternoon John, James, and Peter were walking up and down the foreshore restlessly. Sitting on tufts of grass behind were Nathanael and Thomas and two more of the Eleven, while the remaining four were somewhere in the town. In obedience to Jesus' instructions, they had returned from Jerusalem to Galilee, but he had not appeared to them again. Their lives seemed suspended between the past and an unknown future. The uncertainty bothered Peter, who still had not recovered his natural exuberance and went around like a man who knew he was forgiven but could not forgive himself. John, for his part, had a strong yearning to see Jesus and not to let him go.

As the sun moved into the west, Peter suddenly said, "I'm going out fishing." The others leaped at the idea of activity; even landlubbers Nathanael and Thomas wanted to come. Peter, John, and James spent a happy hour preparing tackle and shortly before sunset the seven put out from the shore. They trawled all night and caught nothing: it was like the night before Jesus had preached from Peter's boat.

At the first sign of the coming dawn, they headed back to shore. When they were about a hundred yards off and dawn was breaking, they saw a Man standing on the beach; the light behind them was too faint to show who it might be. The Man called out to them, "Boys, have you anything eatable?"

"No," they shouted back.

He called out across the water, telling them to cast on the right of their boat, "and you will find." They did not hesitate: a man ashore could sometimes see a shoal invisible to those on the water. They cast a hand net. Immediately, they felt weight and found it already too heavy to draw in.

John knew at once by instinct. Hardly looking up at the figure on the shore, now clearer in the stronger light of full dawn, he said quietly to Peter, "It is the Lord!"

Peter had stripped to work the net. He seized his outer garment, wrapped it round him and jumped into the water and swam toward the beach. John worked the boat inshore, towing the net, and grounded the vessel.

As they jumped out, they saw a charcoal fire. The Man on the shore was cooking a few fish and he had bread too. He said, "Bring some of the fish you have caught." Peter, still soaking wet, climbed back into the boat. He released the net. When the disciples had dragged it onto the beach, they saw an enormous haul; they were astonished too that the net had not broken. Excitedly, they began counting, not merely picking out some to cook, and John never forgot the exact total: 153.

Then Jesus called them to the breakfast he had prepared. As they sat around the fire, the atmosphere was tense; there were no spontaneous greetings. No one dared ask their Host whether indeed he was Jesus: they knew, yet he had an aura about him, of life and power and timelessness, of purity, and a serenity beyond that which comes through suffering. Then he took the bread, broke it, and handed it round, and the fish too; and the tension broke at that characteristic touch of his serving them. When the sunrise flooded the scene with light and warmth, it reflected their joy.

They finished eating. Jesus turned to Simon Peter. "Simon son of Jonah, do you love me more than these?"

"Yes, Lord, you know that I love you."

"Feed my lambs!"

John was happy that Jesus should publicly restore his disciple, John's best friend; but Jesus immediately repeated the question, and when he received the same answer, he said, "Look after my sheep."

Then he asked the question a third time.

Peter looked sad beyond words that Jesus should ask a third time, as if to recall the threefold denial. Peter stood up and walked away, not in pique but in sorrow, and Jesus followed him, and John followed them both. Peter hung his head. "Lord," he murmured, "you know all things. You know that I love you."

"Feed my sheep," said Jesus.

Simon Peter lifted his head. Their eyes met, just as they had met in the high priest's palace less than three weeks before. Peter's sorrow vanished. He accepted the commission to be shepherd of God's flock: no sheep could stray farther than he had. Jesus then gave him a prophetic warning of the martyrdom which he suffered for God's glory thirty-one years later, and repeated the very phrase he had used on the same beach when the four partners had left their nets and the great adventure had begun: "Follow me!"

Several days later they both saw Jesus appear again, not only to the Eleven but to a great concourse of more than 500 believers who had come together somewhere in Galilee on Jesus' instructions. Here was the young man of Nain; and Legion; and a man who once had a withered arm; and another who had been paralyzed, who had come with the four friends who had lowered his pallet through the roof. Cured lepers; once-blind men who now saw; Jairus and his wife and daughter; the woman who had touched the hem of the garment; the Roman centurion, his servant, and his whole household; and scores of men and women who had not been afflicted or distressed but had heard the message which Jesus had preached throughout Galilee. Few were elderly; when the Apostle Paul, who knew many, wrote about the incident some twenty-three years later, most were still alive.

Jesus' words to this company were not recorded, but shortly afterward, he came again to the Eleven on a mountain to which he had directed them. He told them that all authority had been given to him in heaven and earth. He commissioned them to go out and make disciples from all nations, baptizing them, and teaching them to obey all that he had taught: "And be very sure," he said, "that I am with you always, to the end of the age."

From that day onward, the Eleven knew that they were not only disciples but apostles, witnesses of his resurrection, who should begin to proclaim and spread his Gospel to every man, woman, and child throughout the world.

The weeks went by. He appeared to them again and again. Even his half brother James believed, the only opponent to whom Jesus appeared after his resurrection until he stopped Paul of Tarsus on the Damascus road. Caiaphas might speak of a stolen dead body; others might mock, or hint at hallucinations, but John, Peter, and their friends, and James the half brother, knew beyond a shadow of doubt that Jesus was alive, that he was the Son of God, the Christ.

He taught the Eleven more and more about the kingdom of God, and showed in detail how the Scriptures had prophesied plainly what had happened to him. Many matters became clear: why the innocent Jesus had been engulfed by sin as he hung on the cross; why the Baptist, when first pointing him out on Jordan's bank, had said, "Look, the Lamb of God, who takes away the sin of the world"; why the veil of the Temple, which blocked the holiest place, had torn from top to bottom the moment he had died. Jesus instructed them so clearly that Peter, who had been angry when Christ had foretold his crucifixion, learned fast to become a highly effective preacher and witness.

When Jesus ended each time of teaching, he left as mysteriously as he had come, but the apostles were excited at the prospect of seeing him again and did not sorrow.

After five weeks, Jesus told the Eleven to return to Jerusalem, with his mother and other friends. The next great festival, Pentecost, was two weeks away and the city was again filling with pilgrims, but John Mark's family opened their home and the apostles made the Upper Room their headquarters.

Jesus appeared to them while they were having a meal, and ate with them. This time he ordered them on no account to leave Jerusalem. "You must wait," he said, "for the gift my Father promised, which you have heard me speak about; for John baptized with water but in a few days you will be baptized with the Holy Spirit."

On the morning of the fortieth day after he had risen from the dead, Jesus appeared again to the Eleven. This time he led them out of the city by the route of vivid memories which they had taken on the night of His betrayal. As they walked, somebody put a question which the others backed, and thus disclosed that they had missed the point on a vital matter. "Lord, are you at this time going to restore the kingdom to Israel?"

He refused to be drawn. "It is not for you to know the times or dates the Father has set by his own authority," Jesus replied, settling the question so firmly that they dropped the subject and never again confused his teaching about the kingdom. He went on: "But you will receive power when the Holy Spirit comes on you. And you will be my witnesses—in Jerusalem; and in all Judea and Samaria; and to the very ends of the earth."

They walked on. After they had crossed the Kidron Valley, Jesus did not lead them to the Garden of Gethsemane but higher up the Mount of Olives to a quiet spot, without idle bystanders, above Bethany. They stood around him. He gave no farewell, but blessed them in the old familiar gesture, and as he blessed them, his body rose from the earth; the cloud of glory, which had terrified Peter, James, and John at the Transfiguration, enveloped Jesus while they watched. This time it did not terrify: the scene was utterly peaceful.

Their eyes were riveted on the glory as it receded, when

suddenly they saw two men in white, who asked: "Why do you stand looking into heaven, men of Galilee? This same Jesus, who has been taken from you into heaven, will come back in the same way as you have seen him go into heaven."

Then they knew that they would not now see Jesus in physical form, to touch him or eat with him or hear his well-loved voice. They turned back toward the city. But they walked with a light step, not sorrowing nor hopeless but with happiness, because he had ascended to be with the Father, and with a strong expectancy.

They reached Mark's home and climbed the stairs to the Upper Room and told Mary, Jesus' mother, and the other women and friends. All accepted that they would not see Jesus again, but the contrast with the days after his crucifixion could not be greater. Then they had mourned, and felt crushed by the finality of his death; now they rejoiced at the prospect of his promise. They knew themselves to be living through an interlude before the story of his life resumed, and they could only guess at what was coming.

The days went by in mounting excitement. The Eleven and those who knew and believed that Jesus had risen from the dead, a brotherhood of some 120 men and women, met together frequently, praising God in the Temple or filling the Upper Room until there was no space to sit on the floor. They spent time in prayer, remembering his words, "How much more will your Heavenly Father give the Spirit to those who ask him." They talked among themselves. Mary, his mother, could now tell them the story of his conception when she was a virgin, which would have seemed an idle tale indeed before he had risen from the dead. The apostles learned details of his nativity in Bethlehem, and about shepherds and wise men and all the matters which Mary had hidden in her heart until the time came to tell.

Nicodemus could reveal what Jesus had told him when he had gone secretly at night, during Jesus' first visit to Jerusalem after his baptism. It made sense now, that unless a man is born again of water and the Spirit, he cannot see the kingdom of God. And Nicodemus could quote words of Jesus which had mystified him, but now were plain: "God so loved the world that he gave his only begotten Son, that whoever believes in him shall not perish but have eternal life."

They came and went but were very close: Martha and Mary and Lazarus; Zaccheus up from Jericho, bringing the once-blind Bartimaeus; the Jerusalem man who had been born blind; the great counselors, Nicodemus and Joseph of Arimathea; and the numerous party of Galileans. It was from these that they chose a successor to Judas. Peter told them that the choice must fall on one who had been "with us the whole time the Lord Jesus went in and out among us," from the baptism until his ascension. They selected two, and after prayer they took Matthias by lot to become the twelfth apostle, a witness to Christ's resurrection.

By now the broad street outside the Upper Room was becoming busier as Jews and proselytes from countries east and west converged on Jerusalem for Pentecost.

The feast day itself, which originally celebrated barley harvest, was a time for national rejoicing, but for the brotherhood, when they came together early on Pentecost morning, it brought special joy as the seventh Sunday and fiftieth day since Jesus had risen from the dead.

Shortly before 9 o'clock, all 120 were at prayer and thanksgiving in the Upper Room. John was beside Peter. Suddenly an extraordinary noise like the sound of a gale roared into the room. Everybody looked up in awe. The place seemed ablaze, without smoke. Fire separated into tongues and settled on every head. As the flame touched him, John had an amazing sense of being filled with joy and peace beyond anything he had known; a power that almost lifted him. He could see that all the apostles, all his friends, both men and women were being filled; spontaneously, they began to praise God in loud voices and a torrent of words.

Above all else, John had an overwhelming, exquisite feeling that Jesus was in the room—not merely in the room but right within him. Jesus was back, as he had promised: "I will not leave you orphans," he had said. "I will come to you . . . We will come to you and make our home in you."

Jesus had kept his promise. The Spirit had come—the Spirit of God the Father, the Spirit of Jesus himself, and by his coming he made all things new. The old passed away. John was reborn. Peter was reborn. All felt re-created. John could see it on their faces.

Power, fire, joy. Down the stairs and into the street, they cried with joy, praising and laughing, testifying that Jesus was alive. Passers-by and neighbors ran together to see what it was all about. Soon a huge crowd of citizens and pilgrims packed the street, their clothes showing that they came from a dozen or more countries. Only when John heard what the people said, and their looks of astonishment, did he realize that he, Peter and James and the rest were using a battery of dialects and tongues that they had never learned or known before; pilgrims were hearing of God's wonderful works in their mother tongue.

Seeing the crowd, Peter ran back into the house and up-stairs and out on to the flat roof. John followed, and the ten other apostles. Peter put out his hand for silence. Most of the crowd quieted but John heard mocking voices: "They're filled with sweet wine!"

Peter heard, and good-humoredly rebutted the claims. "It

is only 9 in the morning!" he said. "No, this is what the Prophet Joel spoke about: 'I will pour out my Spirit on all people. . . .'" Then Peter preached a tremendous sermon. Listening, John could hardly imagine a greater contrast from the scared slink-away who had lied to a servant girl and denied Jesus, whom now he proclaimed to be Lord and Christ.

Peter spoke of Jesus, his miracles and goodness. He minced no words in reminding his hearers how they had delivered up Jesus to be nailed to a cross: "*But* God raised him from the dead . . . God has raised Jesus to life, and we are all witnesses of the fact. Exalted to the right hand of God, he has received from the Father the promised Holy Spirit and has poured out what you now see and hear."

Peter reached his climax, and John knew that Jesus spoke through him as surely as He had spoken to the crowds in Galilee or Jerusalem. "Let all Israel know for sure," proclaimed Peter, "that God has made this Jesus, whom you crucified, both Lord and Christ."

The sermon went right home. "What shall we do? What shall we do?" cried scores of voices from the crowd. Peter seized his advantage. John thrilled to hear him proclaim the Good News, that everyone who repented and believed could be baptized and receive the same Spirit which had been poured out on themselves. "The promise is for you! And for your children! And for all who are far off—for all whom the Lord our God will call."

Hundreds immediately wanted to be baptized. The apostles worked hard down at the pool, until they had counted about 3,000 new believers on that one single day. And, to the apostles' delight, each of the new believers experienced the same inward sense that Jesus was alive.

For John and his fellow apostles, that Sunday began days

more glorious even than those they had enjoyed with the Master in Galilee. Then, they had been too often stupid, doubting, or disobedient. Now they were fellow workers with him in a new way. They realized that all the Lord Jesus had done and taught in Galilee and Judea was the start of what he planned to do through them and with them, and through those whom he added to their number day by day. John remembered his words at the Last Supper, that they would do greater works than he had done; and with him beside them, they were proving it as they preached and instructed and healed.

It was only the beginning. They would indeed be witnesses to him in Judea and Samaria and the uttermost parts of the earth: Peter would go to Rome, Thomas to India, John to Ephesus and Paul, unknown to them yet, and soon to be their persecutor, would become the hardest working and most traveled apostle of all, after the direct intervention of Jesus.

They knew they were still weak and sinful men. None could compare with Jesus. But the Spirit was making them more like him every day and teaching them. John found that soon he knew the Lord Jesus better than when they had walked together along the lanes of Galilee. He could talk to him more freely in prayer than when they had talked about their needs, worries, or confusions during the months and years when he went in and out among them. Jesus had not only risen but had ascended. He was at the Father's side interceding for them and pouring out his gifts. But he was at their side too.

Each believer, John found, had this sense of growing intimacy. The memory of a great man or a good man will fade with the years, but John already knew the truth that would be expressed a few years later in the immortal phrase: "Jesus

Christ, the same yesterday, today, and forever."

And so John and his friends went out into the highways and byways, the cities and the countryside and crossed the seas to proclaim "the Word of Life, which we have seen with our eyes, which we have looked at and our hands have touched."